Cook

Cook

Thomasina Miers

Easygoing, seasonal recipes

Collins

To my twin, DD, my sister Talulah and to Mark

First published in 2006 by Collins
an imprint of HarperCollinsPublishers
77–85 Fulham Palace Road
Hammersmith
London w6 8jb

The Collins website address is www.collins.co.uk

Collins is a registered trademark of HarperCollins Publishers Ltd

012	011	010	09	08	07	06
7	6	5	4	3	2	1

Photographer: Noel Murphy
Design: Nicky Barneby
Editor: Siobhán O'Connor
Food Styling: Sarah Tildesley, Claire Ptak, Harriet Eastwood

A catalogue record for this book is available from the British Library

ISBN-13 978-0-00-722937-6
ISBN-10 0-00-722937-2

Colour reproduction by Colourscan, Singapore
Printed and bound by Printing Express, Hong Kong

Contents

My food

This book is filled with recipes that I love to cook and that I love to eat. My kind of cooking is all about balancing the two key elements of local, fresh, seasonal produce and a clever arsenal of store-cupboard staples. My kind of cooking is also about embracing and incorporating the twists and tricks of other cuisines. I have travelled extensively in Mexico and elsewhere in South America, in India, in Spain, in France and in Italy. Everywhere I go I pick up ideas, jackdaw-like, that I want to try out at home.

Sometimes cooking is about being creative with whatever happens to be lying around in the cupboard or fridge, and making something that you hope will be delicious for whoever is at home to eat it. At other times, when you are not too busy, it's about choosing the best-looking ingredients from the market or the butcher, and planning a feast around them.

Sometimes I am at a loss as to what to create. I find the easiest way to get around this is simply to go to the shops and see what is on the shelves – maybe something intriguing will inspire me, perhaps influenced by a food article lodged in the murky depths of my head. Or perhaps chatting to the shopkeeper or other shoppers will provide my inspiration. My stock of larder essentials (see page 9) gives me time to shop around for the important fresh ingredients. Farmers' markets and independent food shops offer so much more choice than supermarkets and are often better value. By using them I feel better about how I am spending both my money and my time.

My recipes are influenced by the seasons. Although most of us live in cities or towns, we can still have our pulse on the changing seasons and the origins of our food. Today, as I write, every shop in the throbbing heat of the Uxbridge Road is hawking great slices of watermelon and punnets of soft, summer fruit. I am enjoying the thought of cramming this fruit into everything I can – raspberries into my home-made Pimm's, berries for my fools, softening strawberries whizzed up with sugar to emerge from the deep-freeze in a few hours as an ultra cool and glamorous granita. We are lucky that we have such distinct seasons to make food come alive. It is just as thrilling to get the first gooseberries in late July as it is to get the first quince in November. The wild garlic season is met with delight by all seasonal food nuts like me who try to cram it into every omelette, salad and pesto possible. Or we spend hours having fun thinking what we might do this year with the newly arrived autumnal mushrooms. Even in a concrete jungle, the joy of fresh seasonal remains.

So I like to wait for asparagus to come into season, then really have fun with it, just as I like ignoring the imported stuff at other times of year. This year at Shepherd's Bush market I found slender stalks, which my flatmate and I sliced up and mixed in a delicious concoction of soupy Puy lentils, frozen green peas and a splash of white wine. We ate it with some chicken pieces, pan-fried in olive oil and lemon zest (luckily the chicken was already in my fridge, but the lentils would have done us just as well on their own). The week after, I was in the country where my parents had found some fat, grass-green asparagus grown just down the road and picked that morning, which we gorged on with a rich, buttery hollandaise and some locally baked granary bread and butter. Two weeks after that I was staying in a friend's pub in Brecon where his chef had found wild asparagus that I had never seen before – stems as slender as the inside of a Biro and tips that looked like a wild weed – which he laid under some seared scallops. Utterly delicious and beautifully elegant. I then found some wild asparagus from a mail-order vegetable company, delivered to my door ready for a snazzy dinner for a girlfriend's birthday.

So get to the markets and rely on your senses to taste, look, touch and smell your way to seeking out what's at its very best. Talk to the stallholders, who are very often the best people to ask about how to cook something or to tell you exactly where it has come from. Butchers and fishmongers also know their best buys. I was at my butchers recently and came away with a lamb neck fillet. Long and slender, it cooks in 20 minutes with all the delicious flavour of roast lamb, and when marinated for an hour can take on the flavour of the subcontinent (cumin, coriander, cardamom), the Mediterranean (anchovies, rosemary) or the Moors (sweet paprika, thyme, lemon zest). It looks beautiful sliced on a plate and feeds two people for next to nothing without much work.

My chapters are arranged classically around soups, meat and fish etc. There is a supper section, too, for fun weekend cooking. With many recipes, I give alternative ways to cook a dish or twists that I have found work well. Although I have unashamedly used foreign influences whenever they have excited me, at heart my affections lie with good British produce. The seasonal key (pages 12–13) breaks down all my recipes to their season; however, as you will see, you can always mix and match elements to adapt them to the time of year.

Above all this book is about cooking simple, approachable, great food. Be spurred on by the grins on people's faces when they taste really good food and remember how good you and your body feel when you eat well. I hope you enjoy the book.

A note on seasoning

Seasoning food with salt and pepper is a vital part of the cooking process. Salt brings out the natural flavour in food and pepper gives food a 'lift' in much the same way as chilli. Try to use a sea salt such as Maldon, which is unrefined and free of additives. Season as much as possible throughout the cooking process, tasting as you go along, and you will find you will not need to then pile it on at the table. Seasoning food during cooking allows the flavours to develop, while adding salt to food at the end gives it less chance to bring out the natural flavours of food. So get busy with the salt and pepper from the word go and you will find your cooking suddenly taking on an incredibly delicious flavour of its own.

Tips on sweating

Sweating vegetables over a low to medium heat in olive oil, butter or other fat concentrates their flavour. It allows vegetables to cook until they become soft and slightly sweet, hanging on to their natural juices. It is important not to brown vegetables when sweating them, as their natural flavour becomes tainted and you lose the pure vegetable taste. Covering food in a pan with a bit of greaseproof paper while sweating helps the process by keeping all the moisture locked into the pan. As with all cooking, try it and see.

A note on equipment

The things I really couldn't do without are a pestle and mortar, good, sharp knives, a large, heavy-bottomed, non-stick frying pan, a good spatula and several wooden spoons.

PS I like to cook with olive oil and butter. Eaten in quantity, fat is unhealthy, but in moderation olive oil and butter are key elements to a healthy diet. My grandmother was a successful model. She couldn't have her morning coffee without a spoonful of double cream in it. She wouldn't have dreamed of having new potatoes that didn't drip in minty, salty butter. She would stop eating when she was full, though, and eating sensible amounts of animal fats and oils gave her body its own natural check on its appetite. Stay away from low-fat foods and eat properly. Bodies feel far happier and satisfied with a gutsy salad doused in a delicious olive oil than they do with some mediocre, feeble fat-free salad dressing. If you treat your body well, it will treat you even better.

Larder essentials

I like to have a few key staples in my cupboard so that I can rustle up a delicious, speedy plate of food even if I have only one or two fresh things in my fridge. Cooking is about building up complementary flavours, whether it be with a simple vegetable, a piece of meat or just some pasta. If you have a good selection of oils, mustards, vinegars and spices, you will always be able to build up what you are eating, or give it a little bit of a twist.

So, next time you are shopping, start kitting out your cupboards . . .

Oils

- olive oil – for cooking and frying on high heat
- extra virgin olive oil – for drizzling on salads, vegetables, meat and puddings
- walnut oil – not an essential, but it does do wonders for salads
- sesame oil – for stir-fries, adding an oriental twist to salad dressings, cooking vegetables
- groundnut/sunflower oil – for when you need a mild oil

Note Try to keep your oils stored away from heat and sunlight so that they last longer.

Mustards

- Dijon mustard
- wholegrain mustard
- English mustard

These three mustards have diverse flavours and are good for creating salad dressings and adding zing to different dishes.

Vinegars

Red wine vinegar (body), white wine vinegar (subtle), sherry vinegar (slightly sweet), balsamic vinegar (rich and syrupy), rice wine vinegar (light), cider vinegar (sweet and fruity)

Sauces

Worcestershire sauce, fish sauce, soy sauce, saba, pomegranate molasses, Tabasco, hoi-sin, rosewater

Nuts and seeds

Walnuts, almonds, pine nuts, hazelnuts, cashews, pumpkin seeds, sesame seeds

Tinned foods

Tomatoes (whole plum tomatoes are best), best-quality tuna (stored in olive oil), best-quality anchovies (in olive oil), cannellini beans (for emergencies), butter beans (for emergencies), chickpeas (for emergencies), black-eyed beans (for emergencies)

Dried beans and pulses

Lentils, chickpeas, pearl barley, black-eyed beans, borlotti beans, cannellini beans

Do buy in tins for an emergency, but soaking overnight and cooking your own will give you so much extra flavour.

Spices: the essentials
Cumin seed, coriander seed, fennel seed, cloves, allspice, whole nutmeg, cinnamon sticks, black peppercorns, pimentón (smoked paprika), cayenne

By all means buy some spices in ready-ground form, but it takes just 1–2 minutes to warm up seeds in a dry frying pan, releasing their aroma, and grinding using a mortar and pestle will really lift the flavour. In fact, the difference between ready-ground spices and grinding your own is similar to that between dried herbs and fresh.

Spices: the luxuries
White peppercorns, green cardamom pods, saffron threads, star anise, rose petals, vanilla pods

Spices: if you still have room . . .
Black mustard seed, ground turmeric, ground ginger, poppy seeds

Chillies
Keep dried chilli flakes and dried whole chillies in your larder. Experiment with the different dried chillies now available and ask for them in your supermarket.

- Ancho – sweet and slightly spicy like smoked paprika.
- Chipotle – smoky, fiery and make incredible chutneys, mayonnaises and dressings
- Pasilla – chocolatey, dark, rich, very good with dark meats and game

Bits and bobs
Capers (small are best), dried mushrooms, whole black olives, green olives (stuffed with anchovy are my favourite)

Dried herbs
Bay leaves, thyme, marjoram, oregano, mint, rosemary, basil, sage, dill, tarragon

With the exception of bay leaves, I hardly ever use dried herbs, but they are great in emergencies. Dried mint is particularly good and used in most Middle Eastern cookery. Marjoram is also very handy, as it is difficult to get hold of fresh. Bay leaves are indispensable; dried are good, but see right for my views on fresh bay leaves.

Pasta and grains
Spaghetti, quinoa, couscous, lasagne, angel-hair pasta and shapes such as farfalle and penne

Rice
Brown basmati (nutty), risotto rice (Arborio or carnaroli), Thai fragrant rice (10 minutes to cook), wild rice (mix with ordinary rice, and strictly not rice but a grass), Camargue red rice (for special occasions)

Flour
Plain flour, self-raising flour, '00' pasta flour, polenta, wholemeal flour, granary flour, strong plain flour for bread

Other assorted staples

Baking powder, bicarbonate of soda, good-quality vanilla extract, soft brown sugar, caster sugar (unrefined preferably), molasses, icing sugar, palm sugar, good-quality dark chocolate (minimum 70% cocoa solids), cocoa powder (minimum 70% cocoa solids), Maldon sea salt (for nearly everything), granular sea salt (for flavouring pasta water, cooking vegetables, baking bread etc.)

Fresh staples

Just as you need the basic dried or preserved staples in your cupboard for easy fast food, you will also need basic fresh ingredients.

- Bay leaves – try to find a generous friend with a tree in the garden. A branch tied upside down to a cupboard door will flavour puddings, stocks, stews and sauces until the cows come home.
- Carrot, onion, celery – see box on mirepoix on page 37.
- Fresh ginger root – I drink an infusion of fresh ginger in hot water all the time, either plain, or with a bit of lemon and honey. It does wonders for your circulation in winter and is even said to be an aphrodisiac! More importantly, it adds a delicious, subtle, sometimes fiery note to many dishes. I can't do without it.
- Garlic – I use garlic in almost everything.
- Red onion and shallot – red onion is slightly sweeter than white and looks great in fresh salsas and salads. Shallots are the gentlest of the onion family and add a beautiful subtle flavour to risotto and other dishes.
- Eggs, milk, butter – goes without saying.
- Parmigiano-Reggiano – Parmesan may seem expensive as an initial purchase, but it lasts for months and transforms numerous dishes. If you feel squeamish about spending so much, you can buy Grana Padano instead. Another semi-fat hard cheese, it doesn't cost as much as Parmesan (as you can tell from the flavour, but you won't notice so much when cooking with it). If you are shaving the cheese to eat fresh, though, I would urge using Parmesan.
- Fresh herbs – coriander leaf, thyme, flat-leaf parsley, sage, basil, tarragon, marjoram, rosemary. Fresh herbs are an absolute must in all cooking and some are easy to grow. Sage, rosemary and thyme will last all year in a pot in your garden or on a window ledge. There's nothing like picking some of your own herbs to add to your food to make you feel that you are living the good life. Thyme, marjoram and mint will die down in the winter, but spring back to life again in March/April. Basil generally grows well in a pot in a warm kitchen, but can be difficult to keep going in the winter.

Seasonal listing

This is not intended to be a comprehensive listing of every recipe in the book by season, but my selection of highlights so that you can enjoy the best seasonal recipes in their prime.

Spring

Nibbles, starters and soups
Bruschetta with goat's cheese and spring vegetables 23

Rustic spring vegetable and herb soup 37

Sopa de ajo 36

Watercress vichysoisse 38

Brunches and suppers
Leek, Gruyère and Parmesan quiche 65

Meat, poultry and game
Devilled chicken and potato salad with capers and anchovy dressing 102

Falling-off-the-bone klefticon lamb 90

Leg of lamb stuffed with Middle Eastern rice 148

Roast rack of lamb in Eastern spiced butter 89

Salad of slow-cooked lamb, feta, black olives and dates 86

Slow-cooked spiced butterflied lamb 85–6

Fish and seafood
Mediterranean baked fish 120–1

Sardines escabeche 130

Vegetables and salads
Wild garlic mash 166

Puddings
Rhubarb and custard 194

Summer

Nibbles, starters and soups
Bruschetta with figs, Parma ham and mozzarella 26

Bruschetta with smoked eel, roast beetroot and horseradish 27

Bruschetta with summer tomatoes, pine nuts and basil 26

Gazpacho with toasted almonds 39

Little courgette and dill cakes 30

Summer salmon and mustard seed tartare 21

Brunches and suppers
Pink fir apple potato, roast garlic and tarragon frittata 56

Meat, poultry and game
Braised rabbit with broad beans, rosemary and orange 97

Leg of lamb stuffed with baba ganoush 86

Summer charcoaled spiced lamb with beetroot and horseradish crème fraîche 86

Fish and seafood
Mackerel brandade 127

Pan-fried scallops with summer herb salsa 131

Sardines escabeche 130

Slow-cooked sea trout with verjuice and sorrel beurre blanc 123

Pasta, grains and pulses
Broccoli pesto with penne 158

Lentils with shallots, asparagus and summer herbs 150

Penne with courgette, garlic and toasted pine nuts 154

Quinoa with basil oil and Parmesan 149

Thirty-minute fusilli 136

Thirty-minute fusilli with Serrano ham and manchego cheese 136

Vegetables and salads
Beet, rocket and goat's cheese salad 176

Braised fennel/fennel gratin 156

Broad bean salad with mint, lemon zest and goat's cheese 187

Char-grilled courgette wedges with basil, mint, chilli and lemon 154

Courgette and feta frittata 154

My baba ganoush 159

Pan-fried manchego, watercress and Serrano ham with ripe figs 188

Roast aubergine with tomato, feta and mint 161

Spinach with shallots and nutmeg 157

Warm salad of char-grilled courgettes, feta and rocket 154

Puddings
Blackberry and stem ginger pudding 203

Blueberry and white chocolate pudding 203

Gooseberry fool 204

Gooseberry granita 204

Raspberry and lemon zest pudding 203

Nibbles
and starters

Nibbles, starters, hors d'oeuvres – whatever you like to call them, these have the beautiful knack of shaping the flavour or mood of your lunch or dinner party. The size of a bruschetta can range from a great chunk of bread with delicious ingredients toppling off, to a perfect lunch-time open sandwich, right down to a tiny piece topped with goodies that can be popped straight into your mouth in one go. The ingredients that make up nibbles can be simple and comforting, but still be transformed into a thoroughly elegant canapé. A pissaladière (see page 64–65) is great on a picnic unwrapped from kitchen foil, but also delights when served in a mini tart case with a little thyme and crème fraîche. Chicken liver pâté is as old school as food gets, but is still delectable when done well, served on baby crostini. Many of the recipes in this book serve as brilliant starters in their own right or can be used as alternative toppings for bruschetta (pages 22–7), always drizzled with some delicious extra virgin olive oil.

What's more, nibbles provide a time life-saver to the adventurous cook. I will never be organised enough to have my whole dinner/supper/lunch ready for when the first guest rings the doorbell (the early guest is never a cook's best friend). Instead I rely on putting together plates of goodies for when people are arriving, so that they can start munching on things as they sip their drinks. These nibbles are a moveable feast. Make them substantial in place of a starter or something light to pop in your mouth and whet your appetite. You can then concentrate on getting things finished up, relaxed in the knowledge that you have looked after your guests. Alternatively, offer them nothing and leave them to build up an appetite. All the best things come to those who wait . . .

Smoked mackerel rillettes with a green bean and shallot salad

Smoked mackerel is vastly underrated. Not only is it among my favourite supper dishes, spooned into piping-hot, salt-crusted baked potatoes with lashings of butter, grated mature cheddar cheese (or a Gruyère or Comté) and chopped spring onion, but it can also transform itself into this very quick but classy starter. The rillettes are a rough, loose texture complemented by the elegant and delicious bean and caper salad. Eat as a starter or as a pre-dinner nibble before you sit down.

180g smoked mackerel, skinned

2 spring onions, finely chopped

2 tablespoons chopped flat-leaf parsley

4 tablespoons sour cream

1 tablespoon horseradish cream (see note)

squeeze of lemon juice

For the salad

200g fine green beans, topped and tailed

2 medium shallots

60g small salted capers, rinsed and drained

extra virgin olive oil

squeeze of lemon juice

Using two forks, mash the mackerel flesh in a small bowl. The texture should be loose and rough-looking, which is a lovely contrast to the green bean salad. Stir in the spring onion, parsley, sour cream and horseradish cream.

To make the green bean salad, steam the beans for 7–8 minutes, until they still have a crunch to them. Cool slightly, then combine in a bowl with the remaining salad ingredients. Leave to marinate for 20 minutes.

Serve the mackerel rillettes on plates with the salad, or alternatively serve the rillettes on crostini as with the chicken liver pâté on pages 18–19.

Note You can make horseradish cream by mixing 2 tablespoons grated peeled horseradish root with 100–150ml crème fraîche. Season with sea salt, freshly ground black pepper and freshly squeezed lemon juice to taste. Alternatively, mix a couple of tablespoons of crème fraîche with shop-bought horseradish cream for a better texture and taste.

Crostini

Chicken liver pâté is a classic and always tastes delicious. This particular recipe, used to top crostini, belonged to my grandmother on my father's side. She had an amazing recipe book with snippets of recipes from the 1930s and before. Her butcher in Wales did incredibly thin slices of streaky bacon, which were delicious in this recipe. Crostini, like the bruschetta later on in the chapter, can be topped with so many other things. Goat's cheese and tapenade, the smoked mackerel rillettes on page 16, pesto, the salsa romesco on page 73 with slices of artichoke heart, fresh tomatoes with basil . . . the list is endless. But remember that cooking is supposed to be fun, so don't get so involved with them that they end up taking you five hours. The joy of crostini is that they are quick, easy and bloody good.

Chicken liver crostini

FEEDS A FEW OR MANY, DEPENDING ON APPETITES

5 rashers streaky bacon, chopped

5 shallots, finely chopped

1 bay leaf, crumbled

300g butter, softened

2 small garlic cloves, finely chopped

300g chicken livers, gristle and veins removed, roughly chopped

1 tablespoon port

30ml brandy

1 skinny baguette

good-quality olive oil

sea salt and freshly ground black pepper

small bunch of watercress

hazelnuts, toasted and chopped (optional)

1 tablespoon finely chopped fresh parsley (optional)

Preheat the oven to 190°C/375°F/Gas Mark 5.

Sweat the bacon, shallot and bay leaf in 1 tablespoon of the butter over a medium heat, until the shallot is translucent. Add the garlic and cook for a further minute without letting anything brown. Remove the contents of the pan and set aside. Increase the heat and add another knob of the butter to the same pan. Heat until sizzling hot before adding the chicken liver. Cook for a couple of minutes until the liver is browning nicely on the outside – it should still be pink in the middle. With the heat still on high, add the reserved ingredients to heat through, then pour over the port and brandy. If you like, set alight and flambé for a few seconds to burn off the alcohol (but be very careful).

Remove half the mixture from the pan and blend or process with half the remaining butter. Repeat with the second half of the mixture and the rest of the butter. Blend the two batches together and season to taste.

To make the crostini, slice the baguette diagonally to get long thin oblong slices or slice across for little rounds. Arrange the slices on a baking tray and brush with olive oil. Season with a little salt. Toast in the oven until golden and completely crispy; 5–10 minutes, depending on your oven. These will keep for several days in an airtight container.

Spread the crostini generously with the chicken liver pâté. Arrange on a serving plate with bunches of watercress, scattered with toasted hazelnuts and a little parsley if you like.

Hot pork fillet and romesco crostini

FEEDS 4–6 AS A STARTER

1 pork fillet, fat and sinew removed

1 tablespoon olive oil

2 garlic cloves, ground to a paste with sea salt

grated zest of 1 lemon

1 tablespoon tomato purée

1 teaspoon soft brown sugar

1 tablespoon spice mix
(see page 85)

1 quantity of salsa romesco
(see page 73)

Slice the pork fillet into very thin rounds, no more than a few millimetres thick. Put in a bowl or glass dish and marinate in the refrigerator with the oil, garlic, lemon zest, tomato purée, brown sugar and spice mix for 1 hour. Sear the pork in a piping-hot heavy frying pan for 30 seconds a side to brown the slices. Serve on crostini with spoonfuls of the romesco sauce.

Venison carpaccio crostini

FEEDS 4–6 AS A STARTER

1 fillet of venison

1 small garlic clove (optional)

2 tablespoons salted capers, rinsed and drained

6 anchovy fillets

2 teaspoons Dijon mustard

several good shakes of Tabasco

good shake of Worcestershire sauce

5 cornichons, finely chopped

2 shallots, finely chopped
(about 3 tablespoons)

2 egg yolks

1 teaspoon tomato purée

I had an amazing weekend cooking game with some brilliantly foodie friends. Conor made this delicious tartare with venison fillet, which is incredibly good for you, being a lean, low-fat meat and also full of flavour. Venison is reasonably priced and tender as butter, when properly hung, although I would recommend using farmed venison for this as it is less likely to be tough. Do try this recipe; it takes no time at all and is pretty spectacular.

Slice the venison thinly, then cut each slice into strips. Cut across the strips to make small dice. If you like, chop the meat further for a smooth purée-like dish, but I think it tastes better with some texture to the meat, so I leave it in small cubes, a few millimetres across. Mash up the garlic, capers, anchovy and mustard using a mortar and pestle, then stir in the rest of the ingredients. Next stir into the chopped meat and adjust the flavour to your taste – adding more of any ingredient that takes your fancy. Refrigerate the dish when it is to your liking so that the meat is really cold when you serve it on the salty, crunchy crostini. This is a match made in heaven.

Summer salmon and mustard seed tartare

This is a lovely, summery starter or nibble to give to people in hot weather. It is refreshing but nourishing. The mustard seed bursts flavour into your mouth a little like caviar. Like the ceviche on page 29, you can serve this on crostini or put it in a dish in the middle of the table, letting everyone dive in.

FEEDS 4–6

200ml sherry vinegar

2 tablespoons soft brown sugar

2 tablespoons white mustard seed

300g organic farmed salmon, cut into 1cm cubes

60g pine nuts, toasted and roughly chopped

½ red onion, finely diced

½ grapefruit, segmented and roughly sliced

½ cucumber, peeled, seeded and diced

small bunch of fresh basil, chopped

small bunch of fresh mint, chopped

1 fresh green chilli, seeded and finely chopped

good shake of Tabasco

juice of 1 lime

Using a non-corrosive pan, bring the sherry vinegar and sugar to a simmer. Continue simmering for 6–7 minutes to produce a rich, syrupy vinegar. Pour over the mustard seed and leave to marinate overnight.

Mix all the ingredients together and chill in the refrigerator for 1–2 hours. Serve with crostini (see page 18).

Bruschetta

Bruschetta is the perfect party food. Relaxed, simple and delicious – the only essential is the quality of the basic ingredients. Starting from this basis, always ensure that you have a very good loaf of sourdough or country-style bread that is dense, full of flavour and slightly chewy. A good bottle of fruity extra virgin olive oil is also essential to the flavour of the delicious toasts. See page 159 for my thoughts on this – it is purely a matter of experimentation as to what oil you like best. Armed with these two vital ingredients you have the makings of a blissfully easy starter or nibble that will enthral your guests.

Serving

The way you serve bruschetta is up to you and shapes the mood of your evening. If the loaf is large, serve half slices per person on small plates as a formal starter. Tiny crostini sizes are great fun to pop in your mouth as you are standing around chatting and are dead easy to make from a skinny baguette (although you forgo the sourdough flavour). My favourite way is to have plates on the table for everyone. I then build up the ingredients and seasoning on the toasts and put them all on a large plate or, better still, a beautiful tray. When all the bruschetta are constructed (with as much care given to flavour and appearance as you would show to any other dish), cut into manageable sizes and bring the whole tray to the table. The coloured toppings (beetroot, tomato, feta, pomegranate, figs, black olives, white beans) nestle underneath a carpet of green herbs or leaves (mint, rocket, basil etc.). They look such fun like this and can either be grabbed and munched with people standing around (preferably in another room!) while you finish cooking the main course or served as a relaxed starter at the table with people helping themselves (in the knowledge that there is more delicious food to come).

For the base

Slice the bread and toast it. Rub each slice of toast with the recently cut side of a garlic clove (cut garlic soon turns rancid). Generously drizzle with extra virgin olive oil and add topping.

I like to use a young, peppery, extra virgin olive oil, which adds to the overall flavour of the bruschetta, but do experiment with different types if you feel like it.

Butternut squash, pomegranate and pecorino

This is my favourite bruschetta topping at the moment. It was inspired by April, the head chef at the Spotted Pig, an incredible Michelin-starred gastropub in New York. Go there if you get the chance.

1 small butternut squash, peeled and cut into 2cm chunks

extra virgin olive oil

pinch of red chilli flakes

2 garlic cloves, crushed

1 pomegranate, pith removed and seeds reserved

40g pecorino, shaved

rocket leaves

sea salt and freshly ground black pepper

Parboil the squash in a pan of simmering water until tender, about 15 minutes. Drain and sauté in the same pan in a little extra virgin olive oil with the chilli flakes and garlic for 5 minutes. Add 150ml water and cook the squash until it has formed a purée, about 15 minutes (adding more water if needed). Season with salt and pepper. Toss with the rocket leaves, pomegranate seeds and pecorino, then spread on the bruschetta. Drizzle with plenty of extra virgin olive oil.

Goat's cheese and spring vegetables

200g fresh or frozen baby broad beans

200g fresh or frozen baby peas

100ml extra virgin olive oil

freshly grated lemon zest and juice to taste

4 medium artichoke hearts from a jar, finely sliced

torn fresh chervil, mint and basil leaves

150g goat's cheese

sea salt and freshly ground black pepper

This is a simplified version of the spring vegetable soup on page 37. Parboil the broad beans and peas until just tender, about 10 minutes. Toss through with the extra virgin olive oil, lemon juice and zest, artichoke and herbs. Season to taste. Spread the bruschetta with goat's cheese and top with the spring vegetables.

Poached pears and Dolcelatte

FEEDS 4–6 AS A STARTER

2 pears, peeled, cored and halved

200ml red wine

100ml water

1 teaspoon red wine vinegar

2 tablespoons soft brown sugar

1 cinnamon stick

2 cloves

200g Dolcelatte or Cashel Blue

handful of fresh rocket

Put all the ingredients except the cheese and rocket in a pan and simmer the pears for 10–15 minutes until tender. Remove the pears and simmer the liquid until reduced to a thick syrup. Slice the pears and arrange on the bruschetta with the cheese and rocket, drizzled with the spiced syrup.

Figs, Parma ham and mozzarella

FEEDS 4–6 AS A STARTER

4 ripe figs, quartered

100g Parma ham

150g mozzarella, sliced

1 tablespoon saba (see note on page 167) or balsamic vinegar

extra virgin olive oil

handful of fresh rocket

Arrange the figs, Parma ham and mozzarella on the bruschetta, and drizzle with the vinegar and a little olive oil. Scatter with the rocket and serve.

Summer tomatoes, pine nuts and basil

FEEDS 4–6 AS A STARTER

200g ripe tomatoes, cubed

60g pine nuts, toasted

½ small red onion, finely chopped

small bunch of fresh basil, shredded

extra virgin olive oil

dash of balsamic vinegar

salt and freshly ground black pepper

a little sugar

Toss the tomatoes with the pine nuts, onion, basil, olive oil and seasonings. Marinate for 10 minutes, then serve scattered on the bruschetta.

Smoked eel, roast beetroot and horseradish

FEEDS 4–6 AS A STARTER

450g beetroot, parboiled and diced

pinch of ground cumin

2 tablespoons olive oil

squeeze of lemon juice

100g horseradish root or horseradish cream (see note on page 16)

200g crème fraîche

200g smoked eel fillets

small bunch of watercress

Toss the beetroot in the olive oil and cumin, and roast in a preheated hot (200°C/400°F/Gas Mark 6) oven for 20 minutes. Toss in a little more olive oil and a squeeze of lemon juice while still warm. Mix the horseradish and crème fraîche together. Layer the smoked eel on top of the bruschetta, then scatter with the roast beetroot. Serve with dollops of the horseradish crème fraîche and scattered with watercress.

White bean purée, black olives and parsley

FEEDS 4–6 AS A STARTER

1 x 400g tin cannellini beans

1 garlic clove

juice of ½ lemon

extra virgin olive oil

150g black olives stored in olive oil, roughly chopped

bunch of fresh flat-leaf parsley, stalks removed

sea salt and freshly ground black pepper

Blend or process the beans with the garlic, lemon juice and several good glugs of extra virgin olive oil. If the purée is too stiff, add more olive oil. Season to taste and use to top the bruschetta. Serve scattered with the olives and parsley.

Other possible variations

You don't need to limit yourself to the suggestions above when it comes to bruschetta toppings. For a start, experiment with some of the recipes in this book – and don't forget that drizzle of good-quality extra virgin olive oil. Some favourites include:

- Bagna cauda salad (page 185) – blend or whizz 50g walnuts with an extra 2 tablespoons olive oil in the dressing for some added body
- Jerusalem artichoke, fennel and Parmesan salad (page 178)
- Char-grilled winter vegetables with blue cheese (page 179)
- Pan-fried manchego, watercress and Serrano ham with ripe figs (page 188)
- Baba ganoush (with pitta, hummus and radish) (page 159)
- Char-grilled courgette wedges with basil, mint, chilli and lemon (page 154)

Marinated tuna sashimi with sesame oil and deep-fried shallot

Tuna is delicious raw. It is an endangered fish, though, so buy it only from fishmongers with a good reputation for ethical fishing. Ask them for the tail end, which comes without any of the tough, chewy nerve tissue that runs through the rest of the fish. When you are buying tuna, whether fresh or tinned, it is always best to opt for dolphin-friendly line-caught tuna or skipjack types only. Otherwise we are helping to wipe out their stocks.

FEEDS 4

150–200g fresh tail end of tuna, thinly sliced

1 tablespoon sesame oil

1 tablespoon light soy sauce

juice of ½ lime

¼ teaspoon grated fresh ginger

olive oil

2 shallots, thinly sliced and chopped

1 fresh green chilli, seeded and thinly sliced (optional)

Lay the tuna on a large serving plate. Mix the sesame oil, soy sauce, lime juice and ginger, drizzle over the tuna and cover with clingfilm. Marinate in the refrigerator for 20 minutes.

Meanwhile, pour olive oil to a depth of 2cm into a shallow pan over a high heat. To test whether the oil is hot enough for cooking, drop in a piece of shallot; If the oil sizzles, it is ready. Add the remaining shallot and deep-fry for about 5 minutes or until the shallot is golden.

Remove the shallot from the pan with a slotted spoon and drain quickly on absorbent kitchen paper. Take off the clingfilm covering the marinated tuna and scatter the tuna with the shallot and green chilli, if using. Serve immediately.

Variation
Serve the tuna slices on crostini with dollops of chipotle mayonnaise (see page 69) and the deep-fried shallot sprinkled over the top.

Scallop ceviche

I first tried ceviche in Bolivia after a stint living and working in Chile, although it originates in Peru. It was the most exotic thing I'd ever tasted: fresh, fiery, cooling and bursting with flavour all at the same time. The amazing thing is that it is incredibly easy to make and incredibly good for you. The marinated fish is 'cooked' by the acid in the citrus juices. Do buy extremely fresh fish to get a great-tasting dish.

FEEDS 2

4 or 5 scallops
1 tablespoon thick coconut milk
juice of ½ lime
1 tablespoon chopped fresh coriander
½ avocado, diced and tossed in lemon juice to prevent discoloration
1 teaspoon finely diced fresh red chilli, seeds removed
1 tablespoon chopped grapefruit
1 tablespoon fruity olive oil
a few drops of fish sauce
pinch of soft brown sugar

First put the scallops in the freezer for 30 minutes to firm up. Next slice them across the centre into thin rounds, and put them in a large, flat dish. Toss all the other ingredients together, then toss lightly and loosely into the scallops. Marinate in the refrigerator for 1–2 hours. Serve with crostini or crackerbread as a starter or for people to help themselves to as an hors d'oeuvre (or nibble, as I prefer to call it).

Little courgette and dill cakes

I first had these cakes in a taverna on the Greek island of Samos where I was staying with the wonderful Lemos family. The owner was so busy dancing that my pleas for the recipe fell on deaf ears, but I later got the recipe from Kalliopi. You can make the cakes in advance, then warm them through in the oven. Serve them alone, with tzatziki or on a bed of parsley salad for a starter (see the mackerel recipe on page 126 for the parsley salad).

FEEDS 8 AS A NIBBLE OR STARTER

500g courgettes, coarsely grated

2 eggs, beaten

6 spring onions or 3 shallots, finely chopped

2 heaped tablespoons chopped fresh dill

80g fresh breadcrumbs

100g feta cheese

a little flour

olive oil for frying

sea salt and freshly ground black pepper

Put the courgette in a colander and sprinkle with sea salt. Leave to drain for 30 minutes, then squeeze out excess moisture, patting dry with absorbent kitchen paper. Mix the courgette with the eggs, spring onion, dill, breadcrumbs and feta. Shape into small, flattish, bite-size patties and roll in some flour seasoned with salt and pepper. Refrigerate until ready to cook.

Heat some olive oil in a large frying pan over a medium-high heat. Cook the cakes in batches, frying on both sides until golden – 3–4 minutes a side. Drain on absorbent kitchen paper. You can serve these at once or reheat them when you are ready to eat.

Soups

I love soup. It is fun and fast. It is about grabbing seasonal vegetables and making a delicious concoction with them. Roast some squash, sweat some watercress or whizz up some ripe summer tomatoes. Add some stock and you are ready to eat. Soup was made for easy, seasonal eating.

Warming and comforting, or light and refreshing, soup inspired such passion in me that I ended up spending two years compiling a soup book with a friend of mine, Annabel Buckingham. Most of the top chefs in the country were kind enough to give recipes for it and I was amazed at the never-ending versatility of them. In the process of researching the book I read many other books on soup and talked to masses of people, and discovered that everyone seems to love soup. It can be cheap and cheerful, or incredibly sophisticated. Lyndsay Bareham wrote a staggering 395 pages on the subject. Here are just a few of my favourite recipes for winter and for summer. I do hope you enjoy them.

Just as with any other food, a good soup does depend on good ingredients, although it is sometimes useful for finishing up sad-looking vegetables. Stock is important. Stock cubes are great when you are short of time, but home-made stock will make soup that is in another league entirely. Keeping stock in the deep-freeze is easy: in plastic ½-litre milk containers, larger plastic water bottles or, if you reduce stock substantially, stored in ice-cube trays to emerge as the perfect stock cube. Try to find time to make stock every time you roast a joint of beef or a chicken. The pay-off is well worth what little effort is required – maybe 10–15 minutes of attention to get a delicious home-made stock. It is, of course, not just soup that benefits; added to lentils, pearl barley, potatoes, green vegetables or rice, home-made stock gives you an instantly good, easy supper. Put more exotic ingredients into the equation such as wild mushrooms, asparagus, truffles or seafood, and you are producing first-class dinner-party cooking. So start now to feed yourself and your friends with the quality of food to which you'd like to become accustomed. It really couldn't be easier.

Note If you are cooking a hot soup, always try to serve it in hot soup bowls. Heat them up in hot water, in the microwave or in the oven at its lowest setting. This will ensure that the soup stays hot, rather than arriving at the table tepid.

Chicken stock

Probably the most useful of all kinds of stock, chicken stock will add flavour to anything from a sauce to a risotto or stew, and of course many, many soup recipes, including vegetable broths, provided you are not cooking for vegetarians. If it is really well made you can drink it neat, too. The most obvious way to make a chicken stock is by using the bones and leftovers from a roast. If you are making a stock from a raw fresh chicken, however, just throw the chicken in a preheated 180°C/350°F/Gas Mark 4 oven for 15 minutes to get a bit of flavour in your stock. If you are using a leftover carcass, adding a raw neck of chicken, or gizzard, and some giblets will add flavour and depth.

MAKES 1.5–2 LITRES

1 chicken carcass with all the leftover gunk (skin, fat, jelly, ooze)

1 large onion, or 2 medium, with a few cloves stuck in and cut into chunks

2 carrots, cut into chunks

2 celery sticks, cut into chunks

3 whole black peppercorns

1 bouquet garni or a few stalks of fresh parsley and thyme, and 2 bay leaves

2 unpeeled garlic cloves (optional)

Put all the ingredients in a large pot and cover with water. You want a pot large enough to fit all the ingredients, but with not too much spare room, as otherwise you could drown everything with too much liquid. Bring to a gentle simmer and simmer for 3–5 hours, uncovered, skimming away any grey scum that comes to the surface using a slotted spoon. The impurities in the stock naturally gather in the scum, so this is an easy way to be rid of them. Top up the stock with hot water as the water evaporates so that the stock ingredients are always covered. Strain and cool the stock. Any fat should collect on the surface, which you can then skim off with a spoon once the stock is cool. Refrigerate for up to 3 days covered in clingfilm or freeze until ready to use.

Note Never add salt to a stock in case you need to reduce it later – the more you reduce the stock, the more concentrated the salt levels become.

Tommi's tip

To freeze your stock, pour into old, plastic water bottles or milk containers, and mark the date with a freezer pen. Alternatively, reduce the stock right down after you have strained it to produce a highly concentrated stock. Freeze this into cubes in ice-cube trays to use at later dates. Simply pop a cube out of the tray and drop into your recipe.

Vegetable stock

There are many versions of vegetable stock, but this one is quite gutsy. Use for the base of risotto or vegetarian dishes, or just add some pasta or beans to this broth along with some extra virgin olive oil for a fresh-tasting soup.

MAKES 1.5–2 LITRES

2 tablespoons olive oil

2 large onions, roughly chopped

4 carrots, cut into chunks

3 celery sticks, cut into chunks

1 fennel bulb, sliced

4 cabbage leaves, chopped (optional)

3 garlic cloves, halved

2 leeks, rinsed and roughly chopped

1 bouquet garni (see chicken stock)

a few sprigs of fresh chervil

grated zest of 1 lemon

8 black peppercorns

Heat the olive oil in a large casserole dish over a medium heat and sweat the onion for a few minutes. Add the carrot, celery and fennel, and sweat for a further few minutes. Add the rest of the ingredients and cover with 2 litres water. Bring to the boil and simmer for 1 hour, topping up with water if needed, to ensure that the ingredients are always covered. Strain, cool and refrigerate for up to 3 days or freeze (see tip on opposite page) until ready to use.

Sopa de ajo

I first ate this in the Pyrenees when I was trying to improve my Spanish for A levels. I was doing odd jobs in a bar during the festivities of Semana Santa, and on a particularly homesick day my host made me this soup which he said cured all evils. I have been in love with it ever since.

FEEDS 4

7 garlic cloves, peeled

100ml extra virgin olive oil, plus extra to serve

3 shallots, finely sliced

2 cloves

½ teaspoon pimentón picante (hot smoked paprika)

5 sprigs of fresh thyme

2 bay leaves

12 cherry tomatoes, halved

1.5 litres chicken stock (see page 34) or 50:50 stock and water

splash of sherry vinegar (optional)

2 or 3 slices sourdough bread

4 free-range eggs

100g Parmesan or hard manchego cheese, grated

Using a small pan, cover the garlic with the 100ml extra virgin olive oil and bring to a simmer. Simmer on the lowest heat possible for 25 minutes until the garlic is soft. Remove from the heat and take out the garlic using a slotted spoon. Push the garlic through a sieve and reserve. (You can keep the garlic oil to use for cooking risottos, stews, fried eggs etc. It will keep for several weeks in the refrigerator.)

In a large saucepan, sweat the shallot in 1 tablespoon of the garlic-infused olive oil for 5 minutes before adding the garlic purée, cloves, pimentón, thyme, bay leaves and tomato. Sweat for a further 5 minutes, then pour in the chicken stock. Gently simmer the broth for 30 minutes to allow the flavours to infuse. You may like to add a splash of sherry vinegar.

Just before serving the soup, toast the sourdough so that it is slightly charred. Tear the toast up into bite-size chunks and put in the bottom of heated soup bowls. Check the broth for seasoning, then pour it while still simmering over the toast in the bowls. Carefully break open an egg into each bowl of broth, and serve immediately with a slick of extra virgin olive oil, with the grated cheese in a bowl to hand round the table.

Note The egg will cook in the hot broth, but if your guests are squeamish about runny eggs, poach the eggs in the soup a few minutes before serving or alternatively poach them separately, following the instructions on page 54, before adding to the broth. The Spanish wouldn't dream of cooking the eggs separately.

Rustic spring vegetable and herb soup

This is a glorious spring soup that is fresh-tasting but immensely satisfying. Its taste relies on the quality of the olive oil and stock (and of the vegetables, of course). The great thing is that provided you use baby broad beans you don't need to peel the outer skins, as they give a nice tang to the soup's flavour. If you halve the amount of liquid, you can reduce this down to a delicious spring vegetable ragout to serve over toasted country bread for a starter. Alternatively, adding pearl barley bulks the soup up a bit.

FEEDS 6

150ml extra virgin olive oil

1 large onion, finely sliced

2 celery sticks, finely sliced

4 medium artichoke hearts, finely sliced

1 fennel bulb, trimmed and finely sliced

450g fresh or frozen baby broad beans

200g fresh or frozen green peas

2 baby gem lettuces, finely shredded

1.5 litres vegetable stock (see page 35) or 50:50 stock and water

2 tablespoons chopped fresh chervil

2 tablespoons chopped fresh mint

2 tablespoons chopped fresh basil

sea salt and freshly ground black pepper

freshly grated pecorino to serve

Heat 100ml of the olive oil gently in a casserole pan and add the onion and celery. Sweat gently for 7–8 minutes until translucent. Add the artichoke hearts and fennel, and sweat for another 5 minutes. Add the broad beans, peas and lettuce, and sweat until the lettuce starts to collapse. Pour over the stock and season with salt and pepper. Simmer until the vegetables are soft before adding the chervil, mint and basil.

Serve in warm bowls with slicks of extra virgin olive oil and sprinkled with pecorino.

Mirepoix

Carrots, celery and onion – this holy trinity of vegetables makes an amazing difference to the flavour of stocks, sauces and stews (with the addition of flat-leaf parsley, thyme and bay leaf). In restaurants a mirepoix is an impossibly even, diced combination of these vegetables, with the herbs tied together neatly with string. It definitely needn't be so in your kitchen. I break up carrots and celery in my hands, chop an onion in chunks and throw branches of herbs into simmering water any old how. Then I simply add bones from the butcher, roasted, or leftover bones from a roast for an unbeatable stock. Add mirepoix to any bean or lentil dish in the making to add some real flavour. Sautéed in a little oil, they add body to a stew. Cut them up beautifully and sauté with added fennel, parsnip, garlic etc. as is your wont, to stuff in a tomato, squash or aubergine; or add a piece of bone marrow for a yummy supper dish. Or put them under a piece of fish.

Watercress vichyssoise

This soup has the sharp lemony taste of watercress and is a vivid, bright green if you don't stew the watercress for too long. The secret is to cool the soup in the ice bath soon after you add the watercress (just as you would blanch and refresh vegetables to keep their colour). It is fresh-tasting and dead easy.

FEEDS 6

2 onions, finely sliced

2 celery sticks, sliced

2 floury potatoes, peeled and sliced

2 tablespoons olive oil

1 litre chicken or vegetable stock (see pages 34–5)

400g watercress, or 2 bunches, large stalks removed and roughly chopped

400g baby spinach leaves

Maldon sea salt and freshly ground black pepper

1 egg yolk (optional)

crème fraîche to serve

fresh chives, snipped, to serve

Sweat the onion, celery and potato in the olive oil in a large, heavy-bottomed pan over a medium-high heat until the onion is translucent. Add the chicken stock and simmer for 10 minutes.

Fill a large bowl with ice and a little water, and have another clean bowl ready to fit inside this ice bath, to hold the soup.

Add the watercress and spinach to the soup and let it wilt for a few minutes. Season with salt and pepper, and blend in a food processor until smooth. Pour through a sieve into the bowl suspended on ice. Drop a lump of ice into the soup and stir until it cools. At this point my mother likes to whisk in an egg yolk to give the soup a richer, smoother taste.

Reheat the soup just before serving, taking care not to let it boil or you will lose that carefully kept colour (and curdle the egg if you have used it). Thin down with a little water if the soup is too thick, checking the seasoning afterwards. Serve in warm bowls with teaspoons of crème fraîche on top and sprinkled with some snipped chives.

Gazpacho with toasted almonds

Gazpacho reminds me of summers spent in Spain. It should be made only in the height of summer when the tomatoes have already spent long weeks ripening in the sunshine. It is a refreshing, invigorating soup best eaten on a baking-hot day with a glass of chilled white wine. It can be a complete lunch with some fresh, crusty bread and a slab of cheese to follow, or in small amounts it becomes a light, delicious starter for a party. My favourite gazpacho is a balance of flavours: sweet tomatoes, fiery, uplifting chilli, fresh basil and mint combined with extra virgin olive oil and zingy lemon. This recipe takes 15 minutes – amazing when it tastes so good.

FEEDS 8

60g blanched almonds, toasted and finely ground in a food processor, or 60g ground almonds

900g very ripe tomatoes

1 cucumber, chopped into chunks

1 red pepper, seeds and stem removed

1 red onion, quartered

2 fresh red chillies, seeded

4 garlic cloves

2 handfuls of fresh basil leaves plus extra to serve

2 handfuls of fresh mint leaves

pinch of sugar

300ml passata

100ml extra virgin olive oil

1 teaspoon saba (see note on page 167) or 2 teaspoons reduced balsamic vinegar (see page 80)

2 tablespoons sherry vinegar

good shake of Tabasco

juice of 1 lemon

1½ tablespoons Maldon sea salt

freshly ground black pepper

basil oil to serve (optional)

ice cubes to serve

Combine all the ingredients in a food processor, and process to a rough texture. The soup is great with a bit of bite, so don't overprocess it. Season with lots of freshly ground black pepper.

Serve in individual bowls with a drizzle of basil oil (see below) or a slick of extra virgin olive oil, an ice cube and a few basil leaves. You can also serve this with croûtons, but the soup is very filling so these are not really needed. I prefer to follow it with crusty bread and cheese, and some slices of Serrano ham.

Basil oil

Basil oil makes a delicious dressing to the simplest of salads, frittatas or rice dishes. Drizzle it on baked potatoes, toasted goat's cheese sandwiches or ripe tomatoes. Once you've tried it, there'll be no going back.

Remove the stalks from 3 large bunches of fresh basil (about 80g) and put the basil leaves, 150ml extra virgin olive oil and 1 small peeled garlic clove in a food processor. Whizz up to make a rough oil. The basil oil keeps in the refrigerator for at least a week, but the fresher it is eaten the better. The same oil can be made using fresh rocket, coriander or mint leaves.

Jerusalem artichoke soup with chives and walnut oil

This is one of my favourite soups. It's universally loved and, were it not for people's horrible reactions to Jerusalem artichokes, I'm sure it would be the all-time worldwide favourite soup. Rick Stein, however, has discovered a little trick with Jerusalem artichokes that I have also read about in Madhur Jaffrey books. The Indians are so used to eating flatulence-inducing lentils and beans that over the centuries they have found natural cures. The main one is asafoetida. Add a pinch of this to the soup and you will find that uncomfortable side effects are dramatically reduced. My father was overjoyed at the discovery!

FEEDS 6

6 shallots, finely chopped

2 tablespoons extra virgin olive oil

1 tablespoon butter

1 garlic clove, finely chopped

800g Jerusalem artichokes, scrubbed and roughly sliced

300g floury potatoes such as King Edward or Maris Piper, scrubbed and roughly sliced

pinch of asafoetida powder

2 litres chicken stock (see page 34)

50ml cream

squeeze of lemon juice

2–3 tablespoons walnut oil or truffle oil

2 tablespoons finely chopped fresh chives, thyme or fennel fronds

sea salt and freshly ground black pepper

Sweat the shallots in the oil and butter in a saucepan over a medium heat for 5 minutes, then add the garlic. Sweat for a couple of minutes more before adding the Jerusalem artichoke, potato and asafoetida powder. Sweat for another 5 minutes (adding a little more oil if necessary), then add the stock. Simmer the soup for 20 minutes.

Blend or process the soup to a purée, or push through a strainer until smooth. Stir through the cream and lemon juice, and season with salt and pepper. Serve the soup hot, drizzled with the walnut oil (you can use truffle oil instead if you wish) and the herbs sprinkled over the top.

Black bean soup with avocado salsa

What I love about this recipe is the way the avocado simply melts into the soup.

FEEDS 8

400g black or turtle beans, soaked in cold water overnight

1 small ham hock

2 fresh red chillies, finely chopped

2 onions, chopped

3 tablespoons olive oil

2 carrots, cut into 1cm dice

2 celery sticks, cut into 1cm dice

3 bay leaves

generous bunch of fresh thyme

3 teaspoons ground cumin, preferably freshly roasted and ground (see page 10)

juice of 1 lime

1 teaspoon light soy sauce

2 teaspoons maple syrup or treacle

2 litres chicken stock (see page 34)

sea salt and freshly ground black pepper

For the avocado salsa

juice of 2 limes

2 avocados, finely diced

½ red onion

large handful of fresh coriander leaves, plus extra to serve

1 tablespoon crème fraîche

Put the ham hock in a large saucepan and cover with water. Bring to the boil. Discard the cooking water and rinse out the pan, and remove the skin from the ham hock. Set aside.

Using the same pan, sweat the onion and chilli in the olive oil over a medium heat until translucent, 5–10 minutes. Add the carrot, celery, bay leaves, thyme and cumin, and sweat for a further 10 minutes. Drain and rinse the beans, and add them to the pan, together with the reserved ham hock, lime juice, soy sauce and maple syrup. Season with salt and pepper. Add the stock, bring to the boil and simmer for about 2 hours, or until the beans are tender and the ham is falling off the bone. Allow to cool (which improves the flavour) and skim off any fat released from the ham hock.

To make the avocado salsa (which can be made up to 30 minutes before eating the soup), mix the avocado in with the lime juice so that it doesn't brown, then add the onion, coriander leaves and crème fraîche. Stir through until mixed.

Just before serving, take the ham hock out of the pan, shred the meat and put it back in the soup. Reheat gently and serve in bowls with dollops of the salsa and a scattering of extra coriander leaves.

Chestnut and wild mushroom soup
with watercress cream

This is a rich soup full of flavour and perfect for chilly weather outside. You can make it all year round of course, with dried mushrooms and vacuum-packed chestnuts, but I love the ceremony of peeling my own chestnuts. There's something rather wonderful about it. This soup will fill you up and fill you with cheer.

FEEDS 8

3 tablespoons olive oil

2 tablespoons butter

4 banana shallots (about 250g), finely chopped

500g mushrooms, finely sliced (a mix of wild or seasonal English)

40g porcini mushrooms, soaked in boiling water (optional) and chopped

3 garlic cloves, finely chopped

600g vacuum-packed or freshly cooked shelled chestnuts

1.5 litres chicken (see page 34) or water

small bunch of fresh thyme, leaves picked (see page 000)

2 bay leaves

2 tablespoons sherry

sea salt and freshly ground black pepper

Watercress cream

100g watercress, finely chopped

75ml crème fraîche

juice of ½ lemon

Heat the olive oil and butter in a large soup pan over a medium-high heat. Add the shallot and sweat until translucent, about 5 minutes. Add the mushrooms (if using dried porcini mushrooms, drain them first, reserving the juice to add later) and sauté for 15 minutes to bring out their flavour, seasoning with salt and pepper as you go. Throw in the garlic and chestnuts, sautéing for about 5 more minutes, breaking up the chestnuts with a wooden spoon. Pour in the stock, reserved mushroom juice, thyme, bay leaves and sherry, and simmer for 30 minutes.

To make the watercress cream, whizz the watercress, crème fraîche and lemon juice in a blender or food processor, and season with salt and pepper, bearing in mind how seasoned the soup is. Serve the soup chunky for a restorative, warming supper with dollops of the watercress cream. If you like, you can purée the soup in a food processor or blender for a smoother finish.

Chestnut and chorizo soup

Sam and Sam Clarke do a delicious chestnut soup with chorizo in their *Moro* cookbook. Omit the wild mushrooms and sweat the onion with 200g chopped chorizo sausage. Proceed as for the recipe above, omitting the watercress cream.

Pumpkin, orange and tarragon soup

This is a vibrant, subtle-tasting soup. It has an unusual flavour and makes a lovely starter for a dinner party.

FEEDS 4–6

1 large butternut squash, seeds removed and flesh cut into chunks

3 tablespoons olive oil

3 large onions, finely chopped

½ fresh red chilli, seeded and finely chopped

3 garlic cloves, chopped

700ml chicken stock (see page 34)

400ml orange juice

3 star anise

large bunch of fresh tarragon, chopped, or 1 tablespoon dried

sea salt and freshly ground black pepper

sour cream to serve

Simmer the squash in water until soft, 10–15 minutes. Drain and set aside.

Heat the olive oil in a large casserole over a medium-high heat. Add the onion and chilli, and sauté until slightly soft. Add the reserved squash and the garlic, and sauté gently until caramelised, stirring occasionally (20–30 minutes). Add the stock, orange juice, star anise and tarragon, bring to the boil and season with salt and pepper. Simmer for 30 minutes so that all the flavours can meld.

For a smooth dinner-party soup, push through a sieve. For a more relaxed supper party, remove the star anise and put in a blender. Check the seasoning and serve hot in soup bowls with a dollop of sour cream in each serving.

Celeriac and apple soup

I love celeriac and first found a recipe for this soup in a Jane Grigson cookery book. This one I have adapted for my taste. It is rich and warming, with the tang of the apple lifting the soup to give it a lovely fresh flavour. I like to serve it with a garlic confit cream, but it is delicious without it, too.

FEEDS 6

50g butter

4 apples, peeled, cored and cubed

pinch of sugar

50ml verjuice (see page 130) or a splash of cider vinegar

2 tablespoons olive oil

1 onion, chopped

1 medium celeriac, peeled and roughly cubed (about 700g)

250g potatoes, peeled and roughly cubed

1.5 litres chicken stock (see page 34)

150ml double cream

1–2 tablespoons Calvados or other French brandy

good squeeze of lemon juice

pinch of ground cinnamon

sea salt and freshly ground black pepper

For the garlic confit cream

2 heads of garlic, cloves separated and peeled

150ml extra virgin olive oil

150–200g crème fraîche

1–2 tablespoons very finely snipped fresh chives (optional)

Melt the butter in a large casserole dish over a medium-high heat and sauté the apple cubes, sprinkling with the sugar and seasoning with salt and pepper. When the apple is golden and caramelised add the verjuice and allow to bubble for a few minutes. Remove apple mixture from the dish and set aside.

In the same casserole dish, heat the olive oil and sweat the onion, celeriac and potato for 10 minutes over a low heat. Add half the apple mixture and the chicken stock, and simmer until the celeriac and potato are tender, about 15 minutes. Blend in a food processor, adding water if needed to make a smooth soup. Stir in the cream, Calvados, lemon juice and cinnamon, and season to taste.

For the garlic confit cream, cover the garlic with extra virgin olive oil in a small saucepan and warm gently. The oil should be just releasing a few simmering bubbles. If it starts to simmer too vigorously, remove the pan from the heat for a minute or two, then proceed. Stew the garlic in the olive oil for 25–30 minutes until the garlic is completely soft but not coloured (if it starts colouring, the oil is too hot). Push the strained garlic through a sieve, reserving the oil for other recipes, and fold the garlic purée into the crème fraîche. Season with salt and pepper, and the chives, if using. Chill in the refrigerator.

Serve the soup warm with the garlic confit cream and the rest of the caramelised apple reheated.

Irish soda bread

The easiest bread of them all, with none of that hard kneading involved. The important thing to note when making soda bread is to handle the dough as little as possible. It literally takes a few minutes to prepare the dough, then half an hour to bake. Feel free to add chopped olives, caramelised onions, chopped herbs, cheese toppings or anything else to the basic dough. This recipe makes very good scones, too, if you want your guests to have one each, and they don't take as long to cook either.

MAKES 1 LOAF
375g white flour
75g wholemeal flour
1 level teaspoon salt (granular, not flaky)
1 level teaspoon baking soda
350-410ml buttermilk

Preheat the oven to 230°C/450°F/Gas Mark 8.

Sift the dry ingredients into a bowl and make a well in the centre. Now tip in most of the milk and, with one hand, mix quickly and deftly using a broad circular motion. The dough should be soft, but not too sticky and sloppy. When it comes together, tip it out onto a floured work surface. It's now crucial to wash your hands and DRY them. Flour your hands and pat the dough into a round, tidy shape, then flip over gently onto a floured baking tray. Make a cross in the top of the dough and bake in the hot oven for 15 minutes. Reduce the oven to 200°C/400°F/Gas Mark 6 and bake for another 20-30 minutes until cooked. The bread should sound hollow when tapped on the bottom. If you are making scones, shorten the cooking time by 15-20 minutes so they do not dry out and burn.

Fun brunches, lazy suppers

Some of the best food is created over a lazy weekend, when time is not a factor and you're in the company of good friends. The occasion can be something you have slowly planned over the week, thinking that it would be fun to wake up on Saturday morning with eggs Benedict for breakfast. Or it could be something thrown together at the last minute for an impromptu lunch or supper – maybe a BLT or a frittata, and a bottle of wine, depending on what you have in the fridge and how many people might be popping in.

Alternatively, weekend cooking can mean cooking something that may take a little bit more effort, but that is going to be eaten in the same, relaxed spirit, such as the soufflé on pages 58-9 . It takes a bit more attention than a sandwich, but is essentially a simple-to-follow recipe that takes just over an hour of your time to get on the table. It is one of the most glamorous things to eat. I cook it only for friends who are relaxed about food and aren't put off by my asking for a spare pair of hands to help in the last five minutes. Like a risotto, a soufflé is perfect food for people who love eating but don't stand on ceremony. I find as I get older that I spend an increasing amount of time with people who possess this same attitude to food. Making food is half the fun of the eating experience.

This chapter is full of relaxed food, whether it be mushrooms on toast or a fried egg between two pieces of bread as my sister's all-time cure for too much partying. Buy a Vacherin Mont d'Or in December or January, and heat it up in the oven stuffed with garlic and thyme. Feed it to someone you are keen on and enjoy the fact that the weather is miserable outside. This is food that has nothing to do with price, or the time it takes to cook, but is more about the spirit in which it is eaten. It is about pleasure and enjoyment. Cooking and eating are not a chore or a job; they are a way of life. Don't eat to live; love to eat – it's much more fun.

The best BLT

A BLT – bacon, lettuce and tomato – is without a doubt my favourite sandwich. Cheese-and-pickle comes in a close second. For years, when buying a quick bite to eat, I couldn't order anything else. There is a world of difference between a good BLT and a bad one, though. At home, we like to think we have pretty much perfected the good BLT. The important factor is the combination of slightly sweet tomatoes, salty bacon and lashings of mayonnaise. Oddly, I find only Hellman's will do in the perfect BLT. Home-made mayonnaise just gets lost. Also, if you can find a butcher willing to slice your bacon very thinly for you (order in advance), the flavour seems transformed by using lots of very thin slices rather than a few thick ones.

FEEDS 4

5 tomatoes (1 per person and one for luck), peeled and thinly sliced (see tip on page 136)

good pinch of soft brown sugar

20 thinly sliced bacon rashers (streaky is best)

½ iceberg lettuce, broken up, or 3 baby gems

1 large tablespoon Hellman's mayonnaise

4–8 slices of fresh bread or toast

butter for spreading

Maldon sea salt and freshly ground black pepper

Combine the tomato in a bowl with a good pinch of sugar, Maldon sea salt and black pepper. Let stand for 10 minutes to allow the flavours to meld while you prepare the bacon.

Grill or fry the bacon – the thinner the slices, the better. We like it quite well done with a bit of crunch, but this is a personal preference. Mix the lettuce with the mayonnaise and put in a bowl at the table, with the bacon and the tomato.

Get everyone to sit down and help themselves to fresh bread or toast. The order of assembly is crucial. Begin by buttering the bread and layering on slices of the bacon, allowing the bacon fat to sink into the bread. Next add the tomato, with the juice sinking into the bacon. Finally, pile up the crunchy mayonnaise-laden lettuce. At this stage you may want to top the sandwich with another piece of bread and flip the whole thing over. The tomato juices and mayonnaise make this fairly messing eating, but the flavour is incredible. Alternatively, eat it as an open sandwich with a knife and fork.

Huevos revueltos

These Mexican scrambled eggs are great when you wake up with a ravenous appetite. I like to cook them when I have friends to stay. They are just like scrambled eggs, but with a little kick, and can be addictive. They are delicious served with bacon, in which case cook the bacon first and use its fat to scramble the eggs.

FEEDS 4

8 eggs, whisked

splash of milk

25g butter or lard

1 onion, finely chopped

1 fresh red chilli, seeded

2 tomatoes, skinned, seeded and cubed (see tip on page 136 for peeling tomatoes)

a few drops of Tabasco (optional)

1 tablespoon chopped fresh parsley or coriander

sea salt and freshly ground black pepper

hot buttered toast to serve

Season the eggs with salt and pepper, and whisk in the splash of milk. Melt the butter in a heavy saucepan over a medium heat, add the onion and sweat for 5 minutes. Add the chilli and continue to sweat until the onion is soft but not coloured.

Stir in the egg and cook over a low to medium heat until the egg starts coming together. Add the tomato. Taste the eggs and add a few drops of Tabasco if you'd like. The eggs should still be a little runny, as they will carry on cooking after you have taken them off the heat. Serve with hot buttered toast.

Scrambled eggs with salsa romesco

Try classic scrambled eggs without the onion and chilli, served with teaspoons of salsa romesco (see page 73) on top – delicious on toast for an easy supper.

Tommi's tip

If you find yourself cooking with bacon a great deal, then invest in a little earthenware pot for storing bacon fat (lard). Bacon always renders out a considerable amount of fat in cooking. This fat adds great flavour to dishes when sautéing onions, frying eggs or cooking pancakes.

Eggs Benedict

This is a classic. It is hard to find a really good version of it in restaurants, unless you're at one that takes its food very seriously. Make it at home on a lazy weekend morning and you have the makings of a perfect brunch.

FEEDS 2 FOR A
HEARTY BRUNCH

dash of white wine vinegar

4 free-range eggs

1 quantity of hollandaise sauce (see page 74)

pinch of cayenne (optional)

2 muffins, split in half

25g butter

4–8 slices per egg of any good-quality cured ham (such as Parma or Serrano) or organic smoked salmon

2 teaspoons chopped fresh chives

Maldon sea salt and freshly ground black pepper

Half fill a large, deep frying pan or paella pan with water. Bring the water to simmering point and add a dash of vinegar. Stir the water briskly with a spoon to make a whirlpool in the water and crack the first egg into a cup. Slip the egg into the water and poach for 1–2 minutes. Fish out with a slotted spoon and slide into a bowl of ice-cold water. Repeat with the remaining 3 eggs, transferring to the bowl of cold water each time. Keep the pan of water simmering, ready for when you are just about to serve your eggs. Make the hollandaise as for the recipe on page 74, seasoning with a pinch of cayenne if you like, some salt and some pepper.

When you are ready to eat, toast the muffins and butter them. Put two halves on each serving plate, topping them with the ham. Pop all 4 eggs back into the pan of simmering water for 10–15 seconds to warm through. Drain on kitchen paper and slide over the ham or salmon on top of the hot, buttered muffins. Pour over the hollandaise and sprinkle with chives. Serve immediately.

Tommi's tip

Poaching eggs is very easy when the eggs are fresh – the whites hold together much better than with older eggs. To tell whether the eggs are fresh, fill a bowl with cold water. Drop the eggs in, shell and all, and if they sink to the bottom they are fresh. If they float to the surface or are at a midway point, go and buy some fresher ones.

Talulah's vampire egg sandwich

This sandwich is one of the best hangover cures known to man, along with the Bloody Mary or a glass of ice-cold Coca-Cola. Do not make it if you are attempting to be sociable, as the raw garlic in it won't just be putting off Dracula. It is utterly delicious though and dead easy. My sister Talulah used to make it for me – it's a throwback to her arty days as a tree-hugger in Brighton, when she lived on a strict diet of chickpeas, eggs and garlic. It is an orgy of runny eggs and garlicky mayonnaise. Unbeatable.

FEEDS 1

2 slices of bread (granary is best)

butter

1 medium garlic clove, any green inner stem removed

good-quality mayonnaise

1 or 2 free-range eggs, depending on how hungry you are

handful of chopped fresh flat-leaf parsley

zest of ½ lemon (optional)

slices of tomato (optional)

Maldon sea salt and lots of freshly ground black pepper

Spread the bread generously with butter. Grate the garlic on your finest grater or chop it very finely indeed. Spread the garlic on the bread together with the mayonnaise (just like an aïoli).

Heat a frying pan until it is smoking hot and add a good knob of butter, swirling it around to coat the pan. Crack your egg(s) into the pan and fry for about 3 minutes – until they are turning brown at the edges but the yolk is still runny.

Season the egg with salt, lots of freshly ground black pepper and some chopped parsley. Sandwich into your bread slices with or without the tomato and lemon zest, and devour straight away.

A smarter fried egg with wild mushrooms

Cook the mushrooms as per the sautéed mushrooms on toast (see page 60), using chanterelles in the autumn or morels in the spring. In a separate frying pan, break 1 egg per person and fry as above. Serve the mushrooms with a fried egg on top, sprinkled with garlic breadcrumbs (see page 136), lemon zest and a good squeeze of lemon juice, and a drizzling of extra virgin olive oil. This is a great starter or light lunch dish, but difficult to cook for more than 4 people.

Pink fir apple potato, roast garlic and tarragon frittata

This is a lovely summery dish to eat al fresco. A frittata, just like a Spanish omelette, melds eggs, olive oil and potatoes for perfect picnic eating. Try eating slices of this between fresh baguettes, moistened with some olive oil and tomato, a handful of rocket and a good drizzling of your favourite olive oil (see page 159). Pink fir apples are waxy potatoes with a lovely nutty flavour. They turn a robust dish into something quite sublime, especially with the soft flavours of tarragon and sweet roast garlic. If you can't find pink fir apples, use ratte or other waxy potatoes, as floury potatoes make for a dry frittata. I like this dish cold, as the flavours develop with time and it has a lighter touch if served slightly chilled from the refrigerator.

FEEDS 8

600g pink fir or other small, waxy potatoes, sliced into 2.5cm chunks

1 head of garlic, sliced in half across the middle

extra virgin olive oil

2 leeks, sliced

10 free-range eggs

1 tablespoon basil oil, plus extra for serving (see page 39)

3 spring onions, cut into thirds crossways, then cut into slivers

about 2 heaped tablespoons chopped fresh tarragon

50ml milk

Maldon sea salt and freshly ground black pepper

freshly grated Parmesan to serve

Preheat the oven to 220°C/425°F/Gas Mark 7. You will need a large paella dish or a shallow circular ovenproof dish about 28cm in diameter. Simmer the potato in well-salted water for 15 minutes or until tender. Meanwhile, drizzle the garlic with a tablespoon of olive oil and roast in the oven for 15 minutes. Remove from the oven when cooked, leaving the oven on. Sweat the leek in 1 tablespoon olive oil over a medium heat for 6–7 minutes, until soft but not broken down. Allow to cool.

Break the eggs into a large mixing bowl and whisk together. Season well with salt and pepper. Add the 1 tablespoon basil oil, spring onion and tarragon. Whisk in the milk. Drain the potato and cool for 5 minutes. Squeeze the soft pulp in each cooked garlic clove out of its papery skin into the egg mixture. Beat in well. Add the cooled potato and leek.

Heat the paella dish on the stove until very hot. Add 2 tablespoons olive oil, then pour in the egg mixture. Cook for a minute or two on the stove before transferring to the oven. Cook for 15–20 minutes, until the eggs look just set and the frittata is more or less firm to the touch. If the eggs are starting to brown, cover the frittata in foil until the cooking time is up.

If you are feeling brave, flip the frittata out onto a plate, or simply serve it at the table in the pan. Drizzle with the extra basil oil and scatter over the Parmesan before cutting into wedges. Serve warm, at room temperature or slightly chilled.

A truly sexy cheese soufflé

I learned about this twice-cooked soufflé from Michel Roux Jr, when I had the good fortune of cooking with him during the finals of *MasterChef*. It is quite probably the most decadent food you will ever have the good fortune to eat, a molten cheese soufflé swimming in a pool of peppery, nutty cream. The trick is to whisk your egg whites properly, just as you would when making a meringue or a fool, in a spankingly clean and dry metal bowl, using an equally clean electric whisk (the merest hint of grease really kills a stiff egg white). I cook a giant version instead of individual Gavroche-style ones. It is handy to have an enthusiastic guest to help you to flip the soufflé at the last minute. Apart from that it can mostly be done in advance and should not take more than 30 minutes to prepare and 30 minutes to cook.

Serve simply, with plenty of fruity, white wine and a crisp green salad. Or push the boat out and try it with the shaved artichoke and fennel salad on page 178.

FEEDS 6

50g butter

50g flour

½ teaspoon mustard powder

564ml (1 pint) full-fat milk

240g mix of any hard, mature cheese (Lincolnshire's Poacher is delicious, with equal amounts of Parmesan or Gruyère or Comté), grated

good grating of nutmeg

5 eggs, separated

564ml (1 pint) double cream

sea salt and freshly ground black pepper

You will need a well buttered 2.5-litre soufflé dish, a larger round and shallow ovenproof dish big enough to hold the turned-out soufflé and an oven which has a grill. Preheat the oven to 190°C/375°F/Gas Mark 5.

First, make a simple white sauce (a.k.a. béchamel). Melt the butter in a large heavy-bottomed saucepan over a high heat. When it is sizzling, add the flour and mustard, and stir with a wooden spoon for 2–3 minutes, not minding that it looks totally curdled. Add the milk, bit by bit, stirring furiously with each addition, letting the flour meld with the milk and cook over the heat, to stop your sauce tasting of uncooked flour. When you have added the milk, add just under half the grated cheese, together with the nutmeg and a generous seasoning of salt and pepper, to give your soufflé some punch and remembering that the flavour will be diluted when you add the eggs. Stir to melt the cheese.

Whisk the egg yolks together and beat into the sauce; do not worry if you have any lumps at this stage, as they should soon disappear. Warm the sauce on the stove over a gentle heat, constantly whisking for 10–15 minutes, allowing the yolks to

thicken your sauce, exactly as you would make the custard on page 192, never allowing the sauce to reach boiling point. This is where you can inadvertently make scrambled eggs, so be very careful to remove from the heat whenever you feel it is getting too hot. If you are nervous, have a bowl of iced water to hand so that you can plunge your pan in and whisk like mad if your sauce looks too hot.

You can do all this hours before your dinner and keep the sauce covered with greaseproof or butter paper to prevent a skin forming. Simply warm the sauce 30 minutes before you want to eat, whisking out any lumps that may have formed. At this stage, you can also get your cream ready. Pour the cream into a saucepan and season *generously* with salt and pepper. Simmer for 10 minutes until the cream has reduced by a third and tastes rich and delicious. I like to slightly scald the cream on the bottom to create a nutty flavour like a beurre noir (brown butter). Keep warm.

Thirty minutes before eating, whisk your egg whites using an electric whisk until they form stiff peaks (about 5 minutes). With a large, preferably metal spoon, gently fold a third of your whites into the béchamel to loosen the sauce, then fold in the rest of the whites, taking care not to beat out the air. Turn out into the greased soufflé dish and pop in the oven for 25–30 minutes.

When the soufflé has risen and looks golden on top, get your helper to stand by. Turn your oven to its hottest grill setting, then take out the soufflé and cover it with the larger dish. Flip upside down; it does not matter if the soufflé looks collapsed – this is quite normal. Pour over the hot cream and sprinkle with the remaining cheese. Pop back in the oven until the cheese is brown and bubbling, and smells delectable (less than 5 minutes). Place the finished soufflé in the centre of the table and have fun.

Mushrooms on toast

Mushrooms are a wonderful food. Packed with protein, they pop up all over the countryside throughout autumn and again in spring, and are a forager's favourite. They have a natural affinity with parsley and garlic, and are delicious sautéed on toast. This recipe takes only 10 minutes – yet more proof that good food can be fast food. By all means shell out for some exotic wild mushrooms, but this recipe is also good with chestnut or brown mushrooms. If using the latter, cooking them for 30 minutes over a low heat really releases their flavour, giving them a taste that is uncannily like their wilder cousins.

FEEDS 2

350g mixed mushrooms (wild, chestnut, button)

50g butter

2 garlic cloves, finely chopped

100ml double cream

1 tablespoon brandy (optional)

juice of ½ lemon

handful of finely chopped fresh flat-leaf parsley

hot buttered toast to serve

sea salt and freshly ground black pepper

Remove any dirt from the mushrooms with a brush and cut out any bruised patches. Slice the mushrooms when you are ready to cook (they become dry very quickly if you slice them in advance). Heat the butter in a heavy nonstick frying pan until sizzling. Add the mushrooms and sauté on a high heat. It is important to cook them on the hottest heat or the mushrooms will boil in their own juices – fine if you are stewing them slowly for 40 minutes, but not when you are sautéing them quickly. When the mushrooms are turning brown and have shrunk a little, about 10 minutes, add the garlic and sauté for another few minutes. Add the cream and a splash of brandy, if using. Season with the lemon juice, salt and pepper, and add the parsley. Bubble together for a minute to let the flavours blend and serve on hot buttered toast.

Tommi's tip

You can make garlic parsley butter in advance to store in the deep-freeze. It is then on hand whenever you need it. Leave out 125g unsalted butter to soften. Beat until soft and add a large handful of very finely chopped parsley, Maldon sea salt and pepper. Finely grate in 3 or 4 garlic cloves (add a few thyme leaves, if you like). Mix well and taste – it should be quite highly seasoned. Place the butter on a sheet of clingfilm and roll it into a sausage shape. Wrap in a fresh sheet of clingfilm and freeze. Cut off slices of it whenever you need. Great on steaks, fish fillets and sautéed mushrooms.

Joe's tuna delight with borlotti beans, chilli and extra virgin olive oil

This recipe is a real winner. My friend Joe used to make it for me when we were low on cash and the fridge was bare. He said it was his student tuna dish, taught to him by his Italian grandmother. As long as you have a few tins lying around, you should be able to whip it up in 15 minutes. If you can, invest in really good-quality tuna. Good brands are often sold in delis in glass jars. In any case, you should definitely be looking for tuna that has been stored in oil, preferably olive oil, rather than brine.

FEEDS 3 OR 4

2 tablespoons olive oil

1 medium onion, finely chopped

3 garlic cloves, finely chopped

2 x 400g tins borlotti, cannellini or flageolet beans, drained and rinsed in cold water

2 x 200g tins tuna packed in oil (drained weight)

1 dried red chilli

juice of ½ lemon

splash of white wine (optional)

2 tablespoons extra virgin olive oil

Maldon sea salt and freshly ground black pepper

Heat the olive oil in a saucepan and add the onion. Sweat for 5–10 minutes over a medium heat until translucent. Add the garlic and sweat for a further few minutes, taking care not to burn the garlic. Add the tuna and stir through the onion. Add the beans and 100ml water. Warm to heat through, then crumble over the dried chilli. If you like, add a splash of wine with the lemon juice and let the beans simmer for 5 minutes.

Drizzle with the extra virgin olive oil and season to taste with Maldon sea salt and black pepper. Serve in warm bowls with fresh, crusty bread to mop up the juices.

Salad of borlotti beans with chopped celery and fennel

Chop ½ fennel bulb and 3 or 4 celery sticks, and toss with the recipe above for a delicious salad.

Pasta e fagioli

Add the recipe above to a warm al dente pasta such as fusilli or penne for a variation on the classic Italian dish.

Beans with rich tomato sauce

Follow the main recipe above, adding a 400g tin of peeled plum tomatoes to the onion once it is translucent. Allow to simmer for a good 30 minutes to concentrate the flavours and to get rid of any tinny taste, then proceed with the rest of the recipe. Season with salt and pepper, and a pinch of sugar.

Vacherin Mont d'Or

This is one of the most delicious suppers and takes 5 minutes to prepare. Vacherin Mont d'Or is made only from the milk of cows that graze on summer grasses in the Savioe region in France, and comes in a signature round wooden box. The cheeses are then left to mature for six months before hitting our shops. Vacherin is available only from late November until mid February, so is, unusually, a seasonal cheese. Patricia Michelson, who runs the beautiful cheese shop La Fromagerie, once sent me away with one when I was having a cosy supper à deux. If you wish to inject your love life with a dose of romance, this is the way to do it!

Mont D'Or also comes in a larger size, making it a good supper dish or smart starter for six hungry people when it is served with lots of fresh, crusty bread. Some people like to serve it instead of pudding, as a cheese course, but I think it needs an unspoilt appetite.

FEEDS 2

1 small Vacherin Mont d'Or, around 400g

1 fat garlic clove, halved

small bunch of fresh thyme

1 bottle of chilled fruity dry white wine

fresh, crusty bread to serve

Preheat the oven to 180°C/350°F/Gas Mark 4.

Remove the lid from the box of cheese and make a hole in the middle of the cheese with a teaspoon. Cram in the garlic and thyme stalks. Next, making more space if necessary, pour in a splash of the wine (the rest is for enjoying with your meal). Replace the lid and put in the oven. Cook for 10–15 minutes until the cheese is warmed through and thoroughly gooey.

Serve with the wine, lots of fresh crusty bread to scoop up the molten cheese, a crisp green salad and ripe pears, apples and walnuts to munch on between mouthfuls of cheese.

Pissaladière with thyme and crème fraîche

This tart is French country food at its best. The salty anchovies and rich, buttery pastry offset the flavours of the sweet, caramelised onions. I first tried pissaladière at age fourteen, when I was staying near Grenoble on a French exchange – I was blown away. Not only is it a great supper dish, but it is also wonderful served in elegant slices as a starter accompanied by a fresh green salad.

FEEDS 6-8

For the pastry
180g unsalted butter
240g plain flour
1 teaspoon fresh thyme leaves
pinch of salt
4 tablespoons iced water
a little beaten egg white
uncooked dried beans for blind baking (see note)

For the topping
about 50g butter
1kg onions, finely sliced
2 sprigs of fresh thyme
pinch of sugar
sea salt and freshly ground black pepper
2 tablespoons crème fraîche
2 eggs, beaten
16 anchovy fillets, halved lengthways
about 12 black olives, pitted

To make the pastry, whizz the butter, flour, thyme and salt in a food processor, then add enough water, bit by bit, until the dough just comes together into a ball. Turn out onto a clean surface and bring together, wrapping the dough in clingfilm. Pat down into a flat circular shape and leave in the refrigerator to rest for 30 minutes while you cook the onions.

To make the topping, melt the butter in a large heavy-bottomed casserole pan and add the onion, sugar, salt and pepper. Cook slowly with the thyme for 30 minutes.

Meanwhile, preheat the oven to 200°C/400°F/Gas Mark 6. Roll out the pastry and use to line a 24cm tart tin, pricking all over the base of the pastry case with a fork. Freeze for 10 minutes, to stop shrinkage when you are cooking. Remove the pastry from the freezer and line with greaseproof paper or baking parchment. Fill the tart shell with uncooked butter beans, chickpeas or any other dried bean, and bake in the oven for 12-15 minutes, by which time the pastry should have cooked enough to keep its shape. Remove the greaseproof paper with the baking beans and brush the shell with beaten egg white to seal the pastry. Return to the oven for another 5 minutes until it takes on a pale golden colour. Remove and leave to cool.

When the onion has turned golden and caramelised check for seasoning. Whisk in the crème fraîche and eggs, and pour into the tart shell. Make a lattice shape on top of the onion mixture using the anchovy fillets, and dot with the olives by placing one in the centre of each diamond. Bake in the oven for 10-15 minutes until puffed and golden.

Remove and allow to cool slightly. Serve cut into wedges and accompanied by a green salad for an elegant, classic starter, or as part of a selection of dishes for a fun picnic lunch.

Note Using uncooked dried beans in this way is called blind baking and helps to keep the shape of the tart shell and stop the pastry shrinking too much. You can keep the beans in a tin to use again and again for blind baking other pastries.

Tommi's tip
Try to buy whole olives that still have their stones in and are stored in oil. They will have a much better flavour than the more processed ones that have the stones removed.

Pissaladière with puff pastry

Prepare the onion mixture as above. Roll out some ready-made puff pastry into a circle about 2–3mm thick. Place on a baking sheet and cover with the onion mixture, leaving a 2.5cm border around the edge. Top with the anchovies in a lattice pattern and dot with an olive in the centre of each diamond. Brush the pastry border with a little egg wash. Bake in a preheated 200°F/400°F/Gas Mark 6 oven for 15–20 minutes until the pastry is puffed and golden. Allow to cool slightly and serve.

Leek, Gruyère and Parmesan quiche

Prepare the tart shell as above. Sweat 5 or 6 leeks in 50g butter over a medium heat until soft. Add 2 tablespoons flour, then slowly stir in 200ml full-fat milk, until you have a smooth leek sauce. Whisk in 200ml crème fraîche, 2 beaten eggs, 50g finely grated Gruyère and 50g finely grated Parmesan. Bake in a preheated oven at 200°C/400°F/Gas Mark 6 for 25–30 minutes and serve warm, after the quiche has rested for 15–20 minutes.

Saucy

My love of sauces should be on my epitaph. I nearly drive my flatmate Joe demented – from time to time the fridge becomes so full of glass jars housing mysterious concoctions that he threatens to throw them all out in one fell swoop. At first this passion of mine worried me. Every time I read anything about food it was always about keeping things simple, paring down flavours and letting ingredients speak for themselves. Could I be a real cook if all I wanted to do was create more things to pour over steaks, pastas and steamed vegetables? Then several pennies dropped. Cooking is not about what you ought to be creating, but what you enjoy creating – it is an immensely personal thing and should be relished as such. Secondly, the addition of a sauce to a simple, well-cooked dish can transform it. Think home-made pesto on spaghetti, béarnaise over a fillet steak or hollandaise over poached eggs. And chips are transformed by fat dollops of home-made mayonnaise.

The chimichurri salsa is a case in point. It is found on every restaurant table across the length and breadth of Argentina – a classic South American beef accompaniment that is equivalent to our horseradish sauce. Try it with steak. In an opportune cooking moment, I also discovered it is delicious with lamb and we ate mounds of it with the klefticon lamb recipe on page 90. I'm not sure Greek purists would approve.

Some of the sauce recipes are a cinch to make and just need a whizz in the food processor or blender. Some are slightly more complex, but even with these it is only a question of familiarising yourself with the method, then giving it a go. I used to be terrified by the very idea of hollandaise, but it really isn't hard – just make sure you have a bowl of simmering water to hand to keep the sauce at a steady temperature. It's a real treat poured over eggs Benedict or steamed asparagus on a lazy weekend. Whip up some cream to fold into it and it transforms globe artichokes. If it splits on you the first time, just give it another go.

The salsa romesco is another favourite of mine. I have recently discovered it is delicious on marinated slices of pork fillet for a really fun tapas. Try the recipe on page 19 – it takes a couple of minutes to cook and is a really unusual thing to serve to friends or family with drinks before lunch or dinner.

Home-made mayonnaise

While I am a huge fan of Hellman's mayonnaise (the full-fat version) for certain things such as a good BLT (see page 52) or just for eating with leftover roast potatoes, home-made mayonnaise leaves bought ones standing when you start wanting more from a jar. Once you become creative with mayonnaise it's hard to go back. Start playing around with these variations and you'll soon be in mayo heaven.

2 egg yolks

pinch of salt

½ teaspoon Dijon mustard

2 teaspoons lemon juice or white wine vinegar

175ml extra virgin olive oil and 175ml sunflower or groundnut oil, or 350ml extra virgin olive oil (although this means the mayonnaise will taste quite bitter)

Whisk the yolks, salt, mustard and lemon juice in a china or glass bowl. Slowly drizzle in the olive oil, drop by drop, whisking furiously all the while. Keep whisking, slowly adding all the oil until it is all amalgamated into the mayonnaise.

If you are using a food processor or blender, follow the recipe, adding the oil as the blades are turning. I sometimes like to add a small pinch of sugar to my mayonnaise to balance the bitterness of the olive oil.

Aïoli

Aïoli, or alioli as it is also known, is really just a mayonnaise mixed with crushed garlic. Follow the basic mayonnaise recipe, adding 1 crushed garlic clove to the yolk-and-mustard base. Or add 2 or 3 garlic cloves for an extra garlic hit.

Lemon aïoli

Follow the aïoli mayonnaise instructions, adding the juice of ½ lemon to the yolk base (don't use vinegar).

Anchovy mayonnaise

Mash 4 anchovy fillets with 1 fat garlic clove. Mix with the egg yolk mixture as in the basic mayonnaise recipe above, reducing the mustard to ½ teaspoon and using red wine vinegar in place of the lemon juice.

Wasabi mayonnaise

Add 2–3 teaspoons of wasabi paste to the basic mayonnaise recipe instead of the mustard.

Saffron mayonnaise

Add a large pinch of saffron threads to 2 tablespoons boiling water and set aside to infuse for 10 minutes. Follow the instructions for the basic mayonnaise recipe, adding 1 garlic clove and substituting sherry vinegar for the lemon juice. Add the saffron water when the mayonnaise is made. This mayonnaise is delicious with fish stews and bouillabaisse.

Roast garlic mayonnaise

Put a whole unpeeled bulb of garlic on a baking tray and drizzle with ½ tablespoon olive oil. Roast in a hot oven (200°C/400°F/Gas Mark 6) for 20–25 minutes until the cloves are soft but not overcooked (they turn hard and bitter when overcooked). Squeeze the garlic purée out of the skins and mash up using a mortar and pestle. Whisk into the egg yolk base and proceed as with the basic recipe.

Chipotle mayonnaise

Add 1 tablespoon chipotle en adobo (see page 75) to the basic mayonnaise recipe, omitting the mustard and substituting the lemon juice with lime juice. Taste and add more purée if you like it fiery. Add a pinch of sugar to balance the flavours and serve with prawns, crayfish or lobster for a delicious take on the classic prawn cocktail.

Mojo de ajo mayonnaise
See page 75.

Tommi's tip

A mayonnaise can split if the oil is added too quickly or your blender or food processor gets too hot. If it does split, try adding 1–2 tablespoons lukewarm water bit by bit, whizzing the mayonnaise in between splashes. It should come together. If it doesn't, just put an egg yolk into a clean bowl and whisk it as you add the split mayonnaise, drop by drop. The mayonnaise will come together again.

Hazelnut and preserved lemon pesto

This is a brilliant recipe as the only thing that you need to buy fresh is the mint. It takes 5 minutes to make and is delicious with the stuffed leg of lamb on page 86, or served simply with grilled lamb chops (ready in 12 minutes) or mackerel. Its flavour is most unusual. I sometimes like to add a red chilli to give it a bit of extra kick, not unlike those hot chilli mint sauces that are found in Thailand and Vietnam.

100g hazelnuts

40g fresh mint leaves, stripped from the stalk

1 teaspoon brown sugar

1 teaspoon sumac (see page 186)

pinch of dried chilli flakes

2 preserved lemons, pith and seeds removed

1 large garlic clove, peeled

freshly squeezed lemon juice to taste

100ml olive oil

sea salt and freshly ground black pepper

Put the hazelnuts in a dry frying pan and lightly toast over a medium heat until golden, 5–10 minutes. Warming or toasting will release all the flavours of the nuts (as it does with almonds, walnuts and all those spices such as cumin, cardamom and coriander seed). Don't be tempted to try to do something else while you're toasting the nuts – they will always burn, given the choice. Put the hazelnuts and the rest of the ingredients in a food processor, and whizz until combined. Store in the refrigerator until needed. This pesto will last at least a week, but is best eaten fresh.

Basil pesto

100g fresh basil, large stalks removed

40g pine nuts, toasted

2 garlic cloves

120ml extra virgin olive oil

50g freshly grated Parmesan

sea salt and freshly ground black pepper

Whizz up the basil, pine nuts and garlic with the olive oil in a food processor. Mix in the Parmesan, then season to taste. It is important to season after adding the Parmesan as the cheese is quite salty. Keep in a sterilised jar (see page 85) in the refrigerator with a layer of oil lying on top of the pesto. The oil will preserve the pesto for several weeks.

Note While I love the hazelnut pesto above as a variation of traditional pesto, do try pesto made with walnuts, too – it has a delicious, rounded flavour which is great on pasta or fish.

Salsa verde

Salsa verde, or green sauce, is an Italian herb sauce not to be confused with the Mexican green tomatillo sauce of the same name. It is a beautiful accompaniment to fish, meat and vegetables, seasoned with the saltiness of anchovies and the tartness of capers. It is a creative sauce because, although the classic version is made with only flat-leaf parsley (delicious drizzled over plain boiled potatoes), you can use any green herb you want to flavour the sauce. In this version I have used a touch of basil and mint, but it is also delicious with tarragon when served with fish. I like to mash it up using a mortar and pestle, but by all means use a blender or food processor if you wish, although you will lose the rough texture of the herbs that I love.

2 garlic cloves

5 anchovy fillets

1–2 tablespoons salted capers, drained and well rinsed

1 large bunch of fresh flat-leaf parsley, finely chopped

1 small bunch of fresh basil leaves, finely chopped

1 small bunch of fresh mint leaves, finely chopped

1 tablespoon red wine vinegar

1 teaspoon Dijon mustard

about 100ml extra virgin olive oil

sea salt and freshly ground black pepper

Mash the garlic, anchovy and capers to a paste. Add the herbs and mix into a rough paste. Season with the vinegar, mustard, salt and pepper. Pour over enough of the olive oil to make a spoonable sauce and serve as close to making as possible. The sauce will keep in the refrigerator for a few days, but it does lose its lovely fresh flavour.

Salsa romesco

This is a favourite salsa of mine and goes really well with pork or lamb (see pages 84–5). Try it as an accompaniment to the fish stew on pages 120–1 or just with plain char-grilled vegetables. It is great spooned over scrambled eggs or tossed in pasta and pan-fried prawns or scallops. The thing to do is to make a lot of the sauce and experiment – it keeps for at least 2 weeks in the fridge. It is smoky, fiery, garlicky and sweet all at the same time. There are two ways of making the salsa. You can either have a very rough paste, the consistency of a tapenade, which is made using a mortar and pestle, or you can whizz it up in a food processor to get a mayonnaise-like consistency. Either way the flavours are delicious, and you will find it hard not to keep coming back for more.

6 garlic cloves, peeled

1 large red pepper, halved and seeded

2 large fresh red chillies, stems and seeds removed

4 ripe plum tomatoes, peeled, halved and seeded (see tip on page 136 for peeling tomatoes)

1 large ancho chilli, seeded and torn into pieces (optional)

50g almonds, toasted

50g hazelnuts, toasted

½ piece of bread, toasted

1 tablespoon pimentón dulce (sweet smoked paprika)

1 tablespoon red wine vinegar

180ml extra virgin olive oil

sea salt and freshly ground black pepper

Preheat the oven to 200°C/400°F/Gas Mark 6. Put the garlic, red pepper, chillies and tomatoes in a roasting tin and roast for 30 minutes, taking out the garlic after 20 minutes. The vegetables should be slightly black and charred. If you can get hold of the ancho chilli, omit one of the fresh red chillies and toast the ancho chilli briefly in a dry frying pan, then soak it in hot water for 15 minutes.

Using a large mortar and pestle, pound the almonds and hazelnuts until they form a rough paste. Add the reserved garlic and pound up with the nuts. Now add the toasted bread, tomato mixture and reserved chilli (including the ancho chilli, if you are using), and work into the paste. Season with the pimentón, vinegar, salt and pepper. Work in the olive oil.

Alternatively, whizz all the ingredients in a food processor, adding the olive oil last, drop by drop, as you would when making a mayonnaise. Store in the refrigerator until needed.

Hollandaise sauce

Horror stories about curdled hollandaise abound, but it is not difficult to make ... really. The secret lies in how you are going to eat it. If you are making it for a relaxed lunch with friends, you can whizz it up in front of them, giving them large Bloody Marys to sip on as you cook. It won't take long and you can serve the sauce with your eggs (see page 54) straight away. It's trickier if you are making it for a dinner party that you care about. The sauce doesn't sit well, so if you are not going to use it straight away, keep it in a bowl suspended over a pan of simmering water, to keep an even, warm temperature. If the sauce splits, just whisk in a trickle of cold water and it should come together again.

175g butter, unsalted
2 free-range egg yolks
1½ teaspoons white wine reduction (see below)
squeeze of lemon juice
Maldon sea salt and freshly ground black pepper

For the white wine reduction
250ml white wine vinegar
1 bay leaf
5 black peppercorns
½ shallot, chopped
grating or pinch of allspice

To make the white wine reduction, put all the ingredients in a small pan and simmer until reduced to 1–2 tablespoons. Keep any left over in a jar with a screwtop lid in the refrigerator (for other emulsions such as béarnaise etc.).

To make the hollandaise, melt the butter in a pan. Put the eggs yolks in a glass bowl resting over a pan of simmering water, making sure the water does not touch the bottom of the bowl. Whisk the yolks by hand, or using an electric whisk, until light and fluffy. Add a tablespoon of cold water and keep whisking. Turn the heat off and start adding the butter in a slow dribble, whisking all the time. If you add this too quickly, it will split like a mayonnaise. Do not be deterred, though; it is easy and well worth the effort. Once all the butter is incorporated, whisk in the white wine reduction and lemon juice, and season to taste. Keep over the warm pan while you poach the eggs.

Béarnaise sauce

Substitute tarragon vinegar for the white wine vinegar in the reduction, and add 1 tablespoon chopped fresh tarragon to the finished sauce – made for good steak.

A great sauce for asparagus

Whip 100ml double cream and whisk into the hollandaise sauce for a delicious, frothy mousseline sauce. Perfect with asparagus, this is also delicious with artichokes.

Mojo de ajo

A classic Mexican garlic sauce, variations of mojo de ajo can be found all over South America, France and Spain. To put it in chef's terms, it is almost like a confit of garlic. The garlic is cooked very slowly in olive oil until it turns into a deliciously unctuous caramelised relish. You can make it a week or two in advance, as the oil preserves the sauce. On page 94 I've put it on some pan-fried steak, but it is also extremely good on prawns or pan-fried chicken (see page 103), or used just as a relish drizzled over sandwiches.

2 whole bulbs of garlic, peeled and finely chopped (or use a food processor)

200ml extra virgin olive oil or 50:50 olive oil and sunflower oil

3 fresh red chillies, seeded and chopped, or 1 teaspoon chipotle en adobo (see below right)

squeeze of lime juice

sea salt and freshly ground black pepper

Heat the oil very gently over a very low heat and add the garlic. Cook on the lowest possible heat for 20–30 minutes until the garlic is soft and caramelised. It is crucial not to let the garlic burn or it will taste horrid and bitter. Five minutes before the end of the cooking time, add the chilli. Season to taste with the lime juice, salt and pepper.

Mojo de ajo mayonnaise

Beat an egg in a bowl and season with salt and pepper, and a squeeze of lime. Add the mojo de ajo sauce, drop by drop, until fully incorporated. This is delicious with prawns.

Chillies and chipotles

There are hundreds of different types of chillies in the world. In this book I mainly use the ubiquitous large, fresh red chillies which give colour and a bit of bite to food. Different dried chillies from Mexico lend a huge range of flavour to cooking, but are harder to find so I have stuck with the most common variety, the chipotle. Chipotles are smoked jalapeño chillies and give a smoky, fiery, sweet flavour which transforms snacks and suppers. Buy them mail order or in some supermarkets in a puree called an *adobo*. Mix chipotle paste with olive oil for a deliciously fiery dressing. Dash it into your chilli con carne for an authentic Mexican twist. Make a chipotle mayonnaise to sweet-kick a sandwich or to dollop on shellfish. It makes me want to write a book devoted to chillies.

Fruit alioli

I found a recipe for this in an inspirational book on Catalan cooking called *Catalan Cuisine* by Colman Andrews. This is a delicious adaptation using fruit purée instead of the more usual egg yolk to thicken the sauce and emulsify the oil. The fruit gives the sauce a delicious, fragrant and slightly sweet note.

2 pears or 2 apples or 2 peaches or 1 quince, peeled and cored

4 garlic cloves, any green inner stem removed

250ml extra virgin olive oil or a mix of olive oil and sunflower oil

juice of ½ lemon

Maldon sea salt and freshly ground black pepper

Put the fruit in a small pan and cover with water. Simmer for 5 minutes until soft. Push through a sieve to get a smooth purée. Return to the pan and reduce to thicken, stirring constantly. This process is important as it binds the fruit; without it, your alioli will not thicken.

Using a mortar and pestle, mash the garlic with a pinch of sea salt. Mash in 3 tablespoons fruit purée. Put in a blender and add 3 tablespoons oil, drop by drop, followed by the lemon juice. Beat in the remaining oil in a thin, steady stream. The mixture should be smooth and thick like mayonnaise. Serve with cannellini beans (see page 151) and roast chicken, or drizzled over grilled fish or fresh asparagus in season.

Chimichurri

Chimichurri is a classic steak sauce that is eaten all over Argentina. It is so popular that it is put out with drinks for people to dunk bread into, to munch on before lunch or supper. Serve it with the classic steak recipe on page 94 or use it to dress the falling-off-the-bone lamb dish on page 90.

large bunch of flat-leaf parsley

2 tablespoons red wine vinegar

squeeze of lemon juice

3 tablespoons fresh oregano or 3 teaspoons dried

1–4 fat garlic cloves, depending on your love of garlic

1 teaspoon ground cumin

1 teaspoon pimentón picante (hot smoked paprika)

120ml extra virgin olive oil

sea salt and black pepper

Put all the ingredients in a food processor or blender, and whizz for 3–4 minutes until everything is thoroughly chopped and incorporated. Serve over char-grilled steak. This sauce is best served freshly made.

Meat

Despite being a fanatical salad and vegetable enthusiast I would hate to do without meat in my life. I don't mean that I need to eat it three times a day, but I do relish the flavour of it. I like to buy meat from proper butchers so that I can find out where it has come from, and where I also have access to a cheaper and greater variety of cuts than you tend to find in supermarkets. Skirt steak, pork belly and neck of lamb can be ordered or bought nationwide, and are extremely good value for money. Butchers can also get hold of venison, which is lean and extremely good for you; wild boar, which is rich and full of flavour; and game birds (see poultry section). What's more, meat bought from butchers that is well reared and hung properly invariably tastes better than the mass-produced stuff. I get far more pleasure eating a delicious piece of meat three or four times a week than the cheaper, intensively reared versions twice a day. Great-tasting meat makes great-tasting stock, too, which is a double bonus.

Some of my favourite new recipes are slow-cooked joints of meat, tender and falling off the bone. My version of Greek klefticon is just such a recipe and is the perfect food for a lazy Sunday. Simply pop it in the oven the night before to create a delicious lunch with virtually no work. Stuff leftovers in pitta bread with tzatziki for a fun sandwich lunch. The richly spiced oxtail stew requires 20 minutes more preparation, but again slips into the oven to emerge hours later, rich and warming. It is delicious served over moist polenta in the cold winter months. Both these dishes can be served in between layers of cooked lasagne sheets, too. Just cook the lasagne as you would pasta, then cut them in half. Layer with the soft meat and sprinkle with freshly grated Parmesan. Perfect for a relaxed, slightly different lasagne supper for the family.

There is also fast cooking. Fillets of pork, venison and steak can all be cooked in minutes and are the ultimate fast food. There is little more satisfying than a tender juicy steak – perfect for romantic suppers à deux or for last-minute cooking when you have a few friends to supper. I love fillet steak with wilted radicchio and anchovy mayonnaise, but it is also delicious with the mojo de ajo sauce drizzled over the top. In fact, try a good steak with a number of the salsas and sauces on pages 68–76 and you can have great fun experimenting with the different flavours.

Stuffed pork loin with chorizo, thyme and caramelised apple stuffing

This is a rich dish with a syrupy, fiery balsamic reduction complementing the apple and chorizo stuffing. Cooking the joint separately from the crackling gives you crunchy, delicious crackling and meltingly soft meat. It looks amazing arranged on a large plate and put on the table for people to help themselves. The caramelised apple, thyme and crispy chorizo run through the middle of each slice of pork, with a drizzle of the dark balsamic sauce on top. It's absolutely delicious with greens such as the curly kale on page 164 and nutty brown basmati rice. Serve with the onion relish for a real feast.

FEEDS 8

1 loin of pork (about 2kg), boned with skin scored

1 tablespoon butter

3 apples, peeled, cored and diced

200g cooking chorizo, chopped

2 medium onions, chopped

2 garlic cloves, minced into a paste with 1 teaspoon sea salt

2 heaped teaspoons fresh thyme leaves

2 tablespoons extra virgin olive oil

sea salt and freshly ground black pepper

For the balsamic reduction

200ml balsamic vinegar

½ teaspoon chipotle en adobo (see page 75) or ½ teaspoon pimentón picante (hot smoked paprika)

1 teaspoon redcurrant jelly

200ml chicken stock

string for tying the pork

Preheat the oven to 160°C/325°F/Gas Mark 3. Season the pork inside and out with salt and pepper, and set aside.

Heat the butter in a large frying pan and add the apple, cooking for a few minutes until it starts to caramelise. Toss and cook for a few minutes more until caramelised all over. Remove the apple from the pan and set aside. Add the chorizo to the same pan and fry for 3–4 minutes. Add the onion and sweat with the chorizo until it is soft and the chorizo is nicely coloured and crumbling. Add half the garlic and half the thyme, and cook for a further 30 seconds. Drain the chorizo fat away and mix in the caramelised apple.

Spread the chorizo mixture inside the pork, roll up and tie with string. Brown thoroughly in the olive oil and, with washing-up gloves on, smear the rest of the garlic and thyme into the crackling, seasoning it with salt and pepper. Put the pork in the oven for 50 minutes plus 15 minutes per 500g, basting the joint in its juices from time to time. Twenty minutes before the end of the cooking time, increase the heat to 210°C/410°F/Gas Mark 6–7, to crisp the crackling.

While the pork is cooking, make the balsamic reduction. Put the balsamic vinegar in a small pan and simmer to reduce to about 50ml syrup. When the pork is cooked, remove the meat from the pan and rest in a warm place for 15–20 minutes, covered with foil.

Add the balsamic reduction to the same pan in which you cooked the pork. Add the chipotle en adobo, redcurrant jelly (for sweetness) and chicken stock. Heat through and season to taste with salt and pepper.

Serve the pork in slightly overlapping slices arranged on a long plate, with a little of the sauce poured over and some of the onion relish (below) spooned over if you have made it. It looks wonderful and provides a light, refreshing crunch. Allow people to dig in to more of the relish by having a bowl of it at the table along with the rest of the sauce served in a warm jug.

Pork chops with chorizo, thyme and caramelised apple stuffing

This recipe also works very well with pan-fried pork chops with the stuffing served as a relish on the side.

Marinated red onion relish

This is a classic accompaniment to a whole range of dishes from the Yucatán in Mexico. The red onions are marinated in freshly squeezed orange and lime juice, which draws out the acrid strength of the onion. I loved this relish so much when I was travelling around Mexico that I have since tried it with charcoaled lamb (see page 86), chicken and pan-fried fish, and have found that it is universally good. It is also delicious served chilled on raw food such as tuna or beef carpaccio, steak tartare or marinated fish dishes (see page 28).

2 medium red onions, finely sliced

2 tablespoons freshly squeezed orange juice

2 tablespoons freshly squeezed lime juice

1 tablespoon freshly squeezed lemon juice

1 teaspoon honey

1 tablespoon chopped fresh coriander leaves

sea salt and freshly ground black pepper

Mix all the ingredients together in a non-corrosive bowl and leave to sit for 15 minutes so that the flavours can mingle. Serve at room temperature, or cold from the refrigerator if you are having it with raw fish or meat.

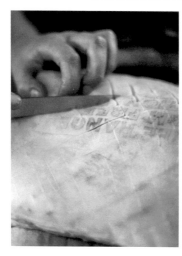

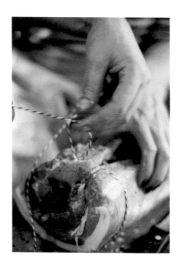

Roast pork with white wine and fennel seed

This is an adaptation from *Classic American Cooking* by Pearl Byrd Foster, a book full of delicious and fun recipes. I do a slower cook than she does and the pork emerges from the oven incredibly tender and fragrant from the fennel seed and herb gravy. This is a great dinner-party dish – it tastes incredible and is extremely elegant. Slice the pork wafer-thin and serve with wild rice and whatever green vegetable is in season. Buttered spinach, char-grilled courgette or steamed purple sprouting broccoli would all be equally delicious.

FEEDS 4–6

1 loin of pork (allow about 150g per person), boned and crackling removed to cook separately

1–2 tablespoons olive oil

a little flour

450ml chicken stock

450ml white wine

1 heaped teaspoon fennel seed

4 garlic cloves, finely chopped

1 tablespoon chopped fresh thyme

1 tablespoon finely chopped fresh rosemary leaves

1 tablespoon finely chopped fresh sage leaves

1 dried red chilli, crumbled

sea salt and freshly ground black pepper

Preheat the oven to 160°C/325°F/Gas Mark 3.

Rub the loin of pork with some olive oil, salt and pepper. Dust with flour and, using a heavy-bottomed pan over a high heat, brown the pork on all sides to seal in the juices.

Pour the chicken stock and wine into a saucepan and add the fennel seed, garlic, herbs and chilli. Bring to simmering point and simmer for 10 minutes to allow the flavours to blend.

Place the pork loin in a roasting pan with half the stock mixture and roast for 45 minutes plus 15 minutes for every 500g. Baste the pork in the gravy every 20 minutes or so. Fifteen minutes before the end of the cooking time, brush the crackling with some of the reserved stock mixture and season with salt and pepper. Put in the oven on the shelf above the pork to heat through.

When the pork loin is done, remove from the oven and turn the oven to its highest setting, to get the crackling crisp. Rest the pork in a warm place for 20 minutes, wrapped in foil. Meanwhile, to make the gravy, simmer the remaining stock mixture in a small pan until reduced by half.

Slice the pork into wafer-thin slices and serve with the crisp crackling and the fennel and herb gravy.

Slow-cooked spiced butterflied lamb

I have been butterflying legs of lamb since first reading Nigella Lawson's tome *How to Eat*. It involves taking the bone out of a leg of lamb and opening up the meat (like a butterfly). This means that the meat has a large surface area, perfect for marinating it with gutsy flavours overnight, so that when you cook it the next day the meat has become totally permeated with the delicious flavours. You can then cook it fast on a barbecue, under a grill or in a hot oven. Or you can do a really slow cook, so that the meat becomes so soft and tender it is almost like butter. This is good with the spinach on page 157 or a rocket salad. I also like it with the pickled beetroots on page 176 and plenty of freshly made horseradish crème fraîche (page 16).

FEEDS 4

1 leg of lamb, boned, butterflied and trimmed of fat, about 1kg after boning (you can ask your butcher to do this)

1 quantity of spice mix (see below)

4 tablespoons olive oil

4 fat garlic cloves, sliced

grated zest of 1 lemon

1 fresh red chilli, seeded and sliced

2 tablespoons maple syrup or saba (see page 167)

2 tablespoons balsamic vinegar

2 tablespoons red wine vinegar

2 teaspoons fennel seed

2 teaspoons coriander seed

2 teaspoons cumin seed

6 green cardamom pods, husks removed

2.5cm piece of cinnamon stick

3 cloves

10 black peppercorns

Mix all the marinade ingredients with the lamb in a sealed plastic bag (making sure there are no holes) and leave to marinate in the refrigerator overnight.

The next day, transfer the lamb (including the marinade) to a roasting pan and roast the lamb in a preheated 210°C/410°F/Gas Mark 6–7 oven for 15 minutes. Reduce the temperature to 110°C/225°F/Gas Mark ¼ and continue roasting for 2½ hours. If you have the time and want a really slow cook, turn down the oven to 80°C/175°F and cook for 4 hours.

Note You can use a boned shoulder of lamb here, as long as you trim off as much fat as possible before marinating and roasting.

Spice mix

Grind up all the ingredients and store in a clean, sterilised glass jar with a screwtop lid (see tip below).

Tommi's tip

To sterilise a glass jam jar, wash it in warm, soapy water, then put in a low (100°C/200°F/lowest possible gas setting) oven for 30 minutes. When making jams and preserves, or storing spices, always use glass jars with secure-fitting screwtop lids.

Salad of slow-cooked lamb, feta, black olives and dates

Marinate 200g sliced feta in olive oil, garlic and seasoning (see page 160). Cook the butterflied lamb as above, then cut into slices. Layer up slices of lamb, rocket or other salad leaves, dates and feta on a plate for an unusual summer lunch dish. Will feed 6 people happily.

Summer charcoaled spiced lamb with beetroot and horseradish crème fraîche

Proceed with the marinade as above. Heat a char-grill or light a barbecue and get really hot. Place the butterflied lamb on the grill or barbecue and cook it 15–20 minutes a side. If it looks as if it is in danger of becoming too blackened, finish off the cooking in a moderate oven (180°C/350°F/Gas Mark 4). Serve with beetroot and horseradish crème fraîche (see page 16).

Leg of lamb stuffed with baba ganoush

Trim the lamb of fat. Create a cavity around the bone of the leg of lamb. Stuff with the baba ganoush given on page 159 and roast in a preheated oven at 220°C/425°F/Gas Mark 7 for 25 minutes. Reduce the temperature to 160°C/325°F/Gas Mark 3 and roast for a further 10–14 minutes per 500g depending on how you like lamb – 10 minutes per 500g is pretty rare; 14 minutes is medium.

Other possible marinades

Moroccan – yoghurt, crushed coriander and cumin seed, garlic
Spanish – pimentón (smoked paprika), garlic, lemon zest, thyme and olive oil
Greek – lemon juice, lemon zest, oregano and olive oil
Classic – rosemary, garlic, thyme, lemon zest and olive oil
Hot – spice mix (see page 85), 2 small dried red chillies and olive oil

Roast rack of lamb in Eastern spiced butter

I was reading Madhur Jaffrey's *World Vegetarian* book and became overexcited by her Ethiopian spiced butter. Different spice mixes crop up in cooking all over the world, but I first grew used to cooking with them when I was at Petersham Nursery under the enlightened cooking of Skye Gyngell. Skye has her own special blend of spices that she keeps to add to all sorts of dishes to bring out their flavours. Spice mixes are delicious in vegetarian stews and aubergine dishes. I particularly like to curry chickpeas (tinned or home-cooked) to make an Indian-style hummus (see page 118) which is delectable with a combination of fried fish and chorizo. Play around with cumin, coriander, fennel, cardamom seed, allspice, peppercorns, cinnamon and cloves to come up with your favourite combination of flavours.

The beauty of this recipe is that, once you have the spices assembled, the dish takes minutes to prepare but looks spectacular when carved at the table.

FEEDS 4

2 x 500g racks of lamb (6 chops each)

sea salt

For the Eastern spiced butter

100g butter, softened

2/3 tablespoon green cardamom pods, cracked and seeds removed

1cm piece of cinnamon stick

2 teaspoons fennel seed

2 teaspoons cumin seed

½ tablespoon black peppercorns

Preheat the oven to 200°C/400°F/Gas Mark 6.

To make the spiced butter, dry-roast all the spices together in a pan over a medium heat for about 5 minutes until the flavours are released, then grind in a coffee or spice grinder (or using a mortar and pestle) and mix into the softened butter. Smear the spiced butter all over the rack of lamb (saving some for the accompanying potatoes) and season with salt. Roast in the oven for 20 minutes.

If you like, cut the racks into individual chops at the table and serve with steamed potatoes smeared in the remainder of the delicious butter.

Falling-off-the-bone klefticon lamb

My favourite Greek restaurant, Halepi, makes a delicious klefticon lamb that we always order without fail. The lamb literally falls off the bone and is incredibly tender. It never occurred to me to cook it at home until a friend, Rachael, telephoned, wanting to cook it for her siblings for a Sunday lunch. We came up with this recipe, which takes 20 minutes to pull together and can then be forgotten until it emerges 9 hours later, soft, falling apart and delicious. It's also great fun to serve it wedged into toasted pitta breads with lots of tzatziki, radish, lettuce and spring onion – perfect to wrap up for picnic grub.

FEEDS 6–8

1 rolled shoulder of lamb, about 2kg, trimmed of fat

40g butter

2 tablespoons olive oil

8 shallots, peeled

6 carrots, peeled and chopped

3 celery sticks, chopped

4 garlic cloves, halved

4 ripe tomatoes, seeded and cut into 8 wedges

250g green olives

5 bay leaves

sprig of fresh rosemary

1–2 tablespoons spice mix (see page 85) (optional)

300ml chicken or lamb stock

200ml white wine or Madeira

sea salt and freshly ground black pepper

Brown the lamb thoroughly in the butter and olive oil in a deep, heavy, casserole dish. Set the lamb to one side and cook shallot, carrot, celery and garlic in the oil until softened slightly. Add the tomato, olives, bay leaves, rosemary and spice mix (if you feel like a more exotic dish). Season with salt and pepper. Stir to mix through, then pour in the stock and wine. Put the lamb back in casserole and bring the liquid to the boil. Cover and put in a slow oven (90°C/195°F/lowest possible gas setting) for 8–9 hours.

Remove the lamb and allow to rest on a carving dish, covered with foil, in a warm place. Strain off the liquid and skim off as much fat as possible – the stock makes the basis of a fine soup.

Serve the lamb and vegetables with rice or floury potatoes. I like to make the meal a whole Greek affair with a Greek salad made with black olives, feta, tomatoes, red onion, cucumber and plenty of freshly chopped marjoram and some yoghurt flavoured with cucumber and mint. You can turn it into a more casual meal by stuffing the meat into pitta bread.

Sicilian oxtail stew with garlic, chilli and a touch of chocolate

Perfect for when you have masses of people in the house and want to be able to whip out a warm, comforting feast apparently effortlessly, this dish is dead easy. It can all be done the day before and cooked slowly in a gentle oven overnight, or cooked the day before, with the flavours mingling and improving in the fridge overnight (as so often happens with stew or soup recipes). I like to bulk up the meat content with a bit of shin of beef. It is flavoured with a little chilli and chocolate, as you find with many good, rich sauces in Mexico, but putting chocolate and chilli with game actually originated in Sicily. Here, you can easily find yourself eating this combination in wild boar and hare ragus with deliciously silky home-made pasta. Make sure the stew is simmering before you put it in the oven, to ensure the meat properly melts into the stew.

FEEDS 6–8

1kg oxtail

1kg shin of beef, cut into bite-size chunks

150g flour, seasoned with sea salt and black pepper

4–5 tablespoons olive oil

3 parsnips, roughly chopped

4 carrots, roughly chopped

10–12 shallots, peeled

7 garlic cloves, peeled and halved

6 celery sticks, roughly chopped

1 cinnamon stick

5 bay leaves

2 or 3 sprigs of fresh thyme

2 or 3 dried red chillies, crumbled

6 juniper berries

10 black peppercorns

1½ bottles rich red wine such as a cabernet sauvignon, a Rioja or a shiraz

500ml stock or water

50g dark chocolate (at least 70% cocoa solids)

sea salt and freshly ground black pepper

Dust the oxtail and beef pieces in the seasoned flour. Heat 2 tablespoons olive oil in a large casserole pan over a high heat and brown the meat all over in batches, using more oil with each batch as necessary and always ensuring that the pan is smoking hot. Reserve.

Heat another 2 tablespoons oil in the same pan and brown the parsnip, carrot, shallot, garlic and celery in batches, too, so that they all become nicely caramelised, seasoning with salt and pepper as you go. When you have finished, put all the vegetables and the meat back into the pan with the remaining ingredients except for the chocolate. Return the pan to the heat to bring the wine and stock up to simmering point.

Meanwhile, heat the oven to 110°–120°C/225°–250°F/Gas Mark ¼–½. Transfer the stew to the oven and cook for at least 3 hours, or even overnight at around 80°–90°C/175°–195°F/ lowest possible gas setting. If you cook this the day before, it will improve in flavour and give you the chance to skim off any fat before gently reheating. When ready to serve, stir in the chocolate, season with salt and pepper (if necessary) and serve with a celeriac mash or mashed potato (see pages 166–7), or a delicious Parmesan-enriched polenta, Sicilian style (page 144).

Steak strips with chilli balsamic dressing

Fun food to serve for friends for a relaxed, cosy evening, as it is pretty messy eating. Order the skirt steak from the butcher – it is a good, economical cut of meat that takes seconds to cook. Skirt steak is used extensively in the Americas but not so much here. If you find it difficult to get hold of, substitute strips of rare fillet steak.

FEEDS 6

½ white cabbage, coarsely chopped

1 large fennel bulb, coarsely chopped

½ red onion, coarsely chopped

1 quantity of chipotle dressing (see page 175)

700g skirt steak

a little olive oil

6 tortillas, warmed

2 avocados, peeled and sliced

large handful of chopped fresh coriander leaves

2 limes, cut in wedges

sea salt and freshly ground black pepper

Put the cabbage, fennel and red onion in a food processor and blitz until you have a shredded salad. (If you do not have a food processor, chop or shred as finely as you can.) Dress with half the chipotle dressing and season with salt and pepper. Set the salad aside.

Slice the skirt steak in half along the grain, then into fine strips (about ½cm wide) across the grain of the meat. Season the strips with salt and pepper.

Heat a large frying pan until smoking hot and add some olive oil to coat. Fry the strips of steak in batches, for 30 seconds on each side. After each batch is cooked, toss the strips in the rest of the dressing in a mixing bowl.

Serve on top of the cabbage salad either on a big platter for people to tuck into or on individual plates. Eat with the warm tortillas, avocado, coriander and wedges of lime on the side.

Vietnamese beef/venison salad

Cook the beef strips as above. Shave carrot and cucumber into a bowl with watercress, torn basil, mint and coriander leaves. Add a handful of halved cherry tomatoes. Toast 60g peanuts in a hot dry frying pan for about 5 minutes, and crush roughly using a mortar and pestle. Toss into the salad and dress with the Vietnamese dressing on page 175. Venison strips instead of beef are also delicious. Follow the instructions on page 96 for cooking venison fillet, then slice up and add to this salad.

Two delicious ways to eat a steak . . .

Char-grilled steak and radicchio with anchovy mayonnaise

FEEDS 4

2 heads of radicchio, stem removed, cut into thin wedges

1 tablespoon olive oil, plus a little extra

1 tablespoon extra virgin olive oil

1 tablespoon balsamic reduction (see page 80) or good-quality balsamic vinegar

knob of butter

4 sirloin or fillet steaks, about 200g each

1 quantity of anchovy mayonnaise (see page 68)

sea salt and freshly ground black pepper

Here char-grilled steak is paired with the bittersweet flavour of char-grilled radicchio. We used to cook this at Petersham Nurseries when radicchio was in season in the walled garden (thanks to Lucy Gray's green fingers). It was an amazing thing to be able to pick it and cook it in the space of a few hours.

Heat a char-grill or ridged griddle pan. Toss the radicchio in the olive oil and season with salt and pepper. Cook on the grill for a couple of minutes a side, until wilted a little and lined with charred stripes. Toss with the extra virgin olive oil and balsamic reduction, and keep warm.

Season the steaks with salt and pepper, and drizzle with a little olive oil. Cook on the char-grill for 3–4 minutes a side for rare steaks; a little longer for medium. Rest for a minute of two, then serve with the radicchio and dollops of the anchovy mayonnaise and a fresh green salad. Heaven on a plate.

Pan-fried steak with mojo de ajo

FEEDS 4

4 sirloin or fillet steaks, about 200g each

30g butter

2 tablespoons chopped fresh coriander

juice of 2 limes

1 quantity of mojo de ajo (see page 75)

Use a good-quality heavy non-stick frying pan here, never cooking more than two steaks at a time or you will reduce the heat in the pan. For a fast, smartish supper, serve with a tin of cannellini beans, drained and warmed through with a couple of tablespoons of a very good-quality olive oil and a squeeze of lemon juice. It is also extremely moreish stuffed into warm baguettes for a lazy weekend brunch. Or omit the mojo de ajo and serve with lots of chips and mayonnaise.

Season the steaks with salt and pepper. Heat a large heavy frying pan for a few minutes, then add a knob of butter and let it sizzle. Fry the steaks for 2 minutes a side for rare steaks and a few minutes longer for medium rare. Serve the steaks with the mojo de ajo poured over the top, with a squeeze of lime and a sprinkle of coriander, accompanied by a crisp green salad.

Ten-minute fillet of venison with juniper berry oil

Venison is now available in most supermarkets and farmers' markets. It is famous for being good for you. Unlike pork, beef and lamb, venison is always very lean, so you can eat it as much as you want without clogging your arteries. The haunch and leg are very good slow-cooked in a rich wintry stew, but the fillet is delicious at any time of year and is incredibly fast to cook. Simply marinate in olive oil and juniper berries for 15 minutes, then fry in a hot pan. The Francatelli sauce takes 5 minutes and was cooked for Queen Victoria by her Italian chef. It goes beautifully with the venison. A delicious, unusual dinner-party dish, ready in no time at all.

FEEDS 4

4 venison fillets, about 200–250g each

100ml extra virgin olive oil

6 juniper berries

1 garlic clove

splash of sherry vinegar

For the Francatelli sauce

1 x 220g jar of redcurrant jelly

2 tablespoons port or 4 tablespoons red wine

1 cinnamon stick

zest of ½ lemon

Put the venison in a glass or ceramic dish. Blend the olive oil, juniper, garlic and vinegar in a food processor, and pour over venison. Marinate for 15 minutes.

To make the Francatelli sauce, put all the ingredients in a small saucepan and simmer for 10 minutes. Transfer to a small serving jug and keep warm.

Pour the marinade off the venison and heat 1 tablespoon of it in a frying pan. When the pan is smoking-hot, add the steaks, two at a time, and sear for 2 minutes a side. Rest for 5 minutes and serve rare with the Francatelli sauce and dauphinoise potatoes.

The venison is extremely good with the bagna cauda salad on page 185. You can also crush 5 or 6 juniper berries using a mortar and pestle, and work into some softened unsalted butter. Season with salt and pepper, and toss through baby new potatoes. This is a lovely accompaniment to venison steaks.

Venison with parsley, tomato and olive salad

Venison steak is delicious with the parsley, tomato and olive salad on page 126.

Braised rabbit with broad beans, rosemary and orange

I love rabbit. It has a flavour a little like free-range chicken. It's a soft, delicate meat that reminds me of the old-school cafés in Italy, where they braise rabbit very simply in olive oil with wine or sage or mushrooms. Rabbit is not expensive and is a brilliant way to feed lots of friends or family. This recipe is a casserole dish, which means you can get it all ready and cook it slowly in the oven while you relax and enjoy your friends. It can be adapted for the winter with a more bolstering prune and mushroom version, but try this on a spring weekend with newly arrived broad beans, some fruit alioli and a delicious salad afterwards – you will feel pretty pleased with life.

FEEDS 6 HUNGRY PEOPLE

2 rabbits, each jointed into 4 pieces

100g flour seasoned with sea salt and freshly ground black pepper

4 tablespoons olive oil

10 shallots, peeled but left whole

2 celery sticks, diced

1 head of garlic, cut in half across the middle

1 orange, halved across the middle

knob of butter

100g blanched almonds, fairly finely chopped

2.5cm piece of fresh ginger, grated

1 tablespoon finely chopped fresh rosemary leaves

1 teaspoon finely chopped fresh thyme leaves

good pinch of saffron threads

2 bay leaves

grated zest of 1 lemon

200ml sherry

500ml chicken stock (see page 34)

200ml fruit alioli (see page 76)

Preheat the oven to 110°C/225°F/Gas Mark ¼.

Dust the rabbit joints in the flour. Heat the oil in a large casserole dish. When sizzling hot, brown the rabbit all over and set aside. Repeat with the shallot and celery, adding more oil if necessary. Sauté the cut sides of the garlic head and orange in the knob of butter until caramelised, and set aside. Next put the almonds, ginger, rosemary, thyme, saffron, bay leaves and lemon zest in the casserole dish, and stir over the heat until the nuts are golden (a few minutes).

Heat the sherry in a small, separate pan. Increase the heat under the casserole to high and add the sherry to the nut mixture, together with the rabbit, shallot/celery, garlic and orange. Light the sherry with a match and flambé until the flames die down. Add the stock, bring to a simmer and put in the oven for 3–4 hours until the rabbit is completely tender. Serve drizzled with generous amounts of the fruit alioli.

This is delicious with slices of toasted, garlic-rubbed sourdough bread. It is also good with the cauliflower purée on page 167, which melts into the sauce. I like to follow this with a refreshing salad of thinly shaved celery, apple and fennel macerated in cider vinegar, or fennel, orange and shredded baby gem lettuce.

Chicken and other feathered friends

I became so horrified by the state of chicken farming a few years ago that I gave up eating it at other people's houses and in restaurants if I did not know it was free-range. There was too much overcooked, intensively reared meat in restaurants giving the bird a bad name. Chicken doesn't have to be that way and restaurants have realised that people want to know where their meat has come from and if it has had a happy life. Rear a bird in its natural habitat and you will taste the difference. There is nothing more satisfying than pulling a fat free-range chicken from a hot oven, sizzling and filling the kitchen with the smells of garlic, thyme and tarragon. Roast chicken is a dish fit for kings. Try the classic recipe on page 100 and serve it on a bed of saffron cannellini beans (see page 151), drizzled with fruit alioli. This is comfort food at its best. You will pay more for a free-range bird, but if nothing else the amazingly high fat content of intensively reared birds should deter one from ever buying them again. With well-reared birds you will get much richer, tastier meat, perfect for all kinds of leftover dishes (the salad on page 102 is one of my favourite ways of using up leftover chicken). You will also be able to get a marvellous stock from the carcass – one that wobbles and jellies like all good stocks should. (I grew up with my grandmother telling me that the jelly contains all the goodness from the bones – how right she was. I think the jelly is the surefire proof of a good pork pie.) Stock is a doddle to make and provides the basis for so many delicious recipes – soups, risottos, sauces, stews. It is nutritious and low in fat, and incredibly satisfying.

I am also thrilled that game is making a comeback. It is a great free-range food, very good value for money and really versatile. Whether pot-roasting pheasant with fragrant spices and coconut milk, or roasting partridge with mascarpone, apricots and marjoram, there are so many ways of getting creative in the kitchen. Supermarkets and farmers' markets are now awake to the increasing demand for game and it is now very easy to buy. You can even order it direct from estates up and down the country. Just get sleuthing on the Internet and bag yourself some supper.

Roast tarragon chicken with saffron cannellini beans

Roast chicken is one of life's treats and one of my favourite things to eat. In this recipe I smear the cavity between the flesh and the skin with tarragon butter. Chicken and tarragon are a match made in heaven, a natural partnership like lamb and mint sauce, beef and horseradish, sausages and mustard. The tarragon butter melts into the flesh and more tarragon is stuffed inside the chicken. It is delicious and looks spectacular taken to the table sitting on a bed of saffron cannellini beans, drizzled with fruit alioli.

FEEDS 6

1 medium free-range chicken, about 1.5kg

50g butter

½ onion

½ lemon

2 garlic cloves, smashed with the back of a knife

6 large sprigs of fresh tarragon

3 sprigs of fresh thyme

½ glass white wine

sea salt and freshly ground black pepper

For the tarragon butter

1 heaped tablespoon chopped fresh tarragon

1 garlic clove, finely chopped

50g butter, softened

Preheat the oven to 220°C/425°F/Gas Mark 7. Season the chicken inside and out with plenty of salt and pepper. This is important and will add to the flavour of the cooked bird. Stuff the chicken with the butter, onion, lemon and flattened garlic cloves. Add the tarragon and thyme.

To make the tarragon butter, process all the ingredients in a food processor and season with salt and pepper. Prise the skin away from the chicken breast and all the way down to the chicken leg, being careful not to tear it. Smear the tarragon butter in between the flesh and skin of the bird. Prise the legs a little way away from the carcass, too, so that the legs cook more in time with the rest of the bird. Pour half the wine into a roasting dish.

Roast the chicken in the oven for 15 minutes. Pour the rest of the wine into the pan and continue cooking for 30 minutes per kg with the oven turned down to 180°C/350°F/Gas Mark 4. When the time is up insert a skewer into the thigh. The juices should run clear. If the meat is still pink, cook a little more. Leave to rest for 20 minutes in a warm place, covered with foil. This will relax the meat, tenderising it and allowing the juices to flow back into the flesh. Serve carved in joints on a bed of saffron cannellini beans (see page 151), drizzled in fruit alioli (page 76).

Devilled chicken and potato salad with capers and anchovy dressing

Leftover chicken has many uses, but this one I discovered when I had to find a use for leftover turkey for a column I did last Christmas. A really good coronation chicken or cold chicken in a baguette with masses of mayonnaise (see pages 68-9) proves that cold chicken is brilliant fast food. I used to devil it when I was little, and I tried this method the other day, using olive oil instead of butter. I added it to a sort of Caesar salad – leftovers fit for a king and you should have the ingredients lying around in your cupboard. The salad is gutsy, combining delicious, mustardy, fiery bits of chicken with crisp Cos lettuce, capers and potatoes tossed in the garlic anchovy dressing. Yum.

FEEDS 6

500g cooked chicken, cut into chunks

300-350g waxy potatoes, cut into equal-sized chunks

½ cos lettuce or 3 baby gems

2 tablespoons salted capers, rinsed, drained and chopped

For the devilling

4 teaspoons Colman's mustard powder

a few generous dashes of Worcestershire sauce

good pinch of dried crumbled chillies (or more if you like it hot!)

3 tablespoons olive oil

For the anchovy dressing

2 anchovy fillets

1 garlic clove, peeled

pinch of sugar

½ teaspoon Dijon mustard

1 tablespoon red wine vinegar

120ml extra virgin olive oil

1-2 tablespoons freshly grated Parmesan

sea salt and freshly ground black pepper

To make the anchovy dressing, mash the anchovy and garlic together with the salt, pepper and sugar, then gradually mix in the rest of the ingredients. You want a thick, gutsy dressing.

Boil the potatoes and, when they are tender and still warm, toss them in half the salad dressing so that they soak up all the flavour. Meanwhile, mix together the devilish dressing and toss into the chicken meat so that it all has a generous coating. Heat a large frying pan until smoking hot, toss in the chicken and fry for a good 4-5 minutes to get a crispy, browned coating, turning the heat down if the chicken starts to brown too much. Fry on the other side until nicely browned, then set aside to cool slightly.

To serve, toss the crunchy lettuce leaves with the devilled chicken, capers, potato and the rest of the dressing, and put into a salad bowl. Plonk on the table and tuck in.

Variation

Stuff the devilled chicken into a crusty baguette with some iceberg lettuce and lots of mayonnaise (pounded with a bit of garlic and anchovy if you can be bothered – see recipe for anchovy mayo on page 68) and you have the perfect hot lunchtime sandwich.

Pan-fried chicken with walnut sauce

This walnut sauce is inspired by the Middle Eastern walnut 'tarator' sauce I once had at Moro and loved so much. I adore walnuts – not only are they good for you (see page 178), but they are such an easy, healthy snack as well. Their deliciously creamy flavour really comes through in this sauce. The paste can also be used for other snacks and suppers. Pan-fry a fillet of John dory and serve it with spinach in the walnut sauce for a healthy, fast and glamorous dinner for two.

FEEDS 4

4 free-range chicken breasts with skin on, or 8 small chicken pieces
1 tablespoon butter
50ml red wine
150ml chicken stock (see page 34)
sprig of fresh thyme
sea salt and freshly ground black pepper

For the walnut sauce

150g walnuts
1 slice of toast
1 fat garlic clove
2 teaspoons red wine vinegar
juice of ½ lemon
½ teaspoon ground cumin
good pinch of sugar
100ml extra virgin olive oil

Preheat the oven to 180°C/350°F/Gas Mark 4. Season the chicken with salt and pepper, and set aside. (Seasoning early will increase the flavour of the chicken when you cook it.)

To make the walnut sauce, grind up the walnuts in a food processor for about 2 minutes until paste-like. Add the toast, garlic, vinegar, lemon juice, cumin, sugar and olive oil, and whizz some more. Taste for seasoning, adding salt and pepper if necessary. Don't worry if the sauce looks separated at this stage – it will all come together.

Heat a large frying pan until smoking hot and add the butter. Add the chicken skin side down and fry for 4–5 minutes to get a delicious, crispy skin. Turn over and fry for another 2 minutes, pop onto a hot baking tray skin side down and finish off in the oven for 2 more minutes. Rest on a warm plate. Meanwhile, add 2 tablespoons of the walnut paste to the pan and cook over a medium-high heat for a minute. Add the wine, stock and thyme, and simmer to reduce to a thick, creamy sauce. Stir 3 more tablespoons of the walnut paste into the sauce and pour over the reserved chicken.

This is delicious with plain boiled potatoes or green coriander rice (see page 148). I like to follow this dish with a fresh green salad. You could make just as delicious a sauce with white wine for a full-bodied fish such as monkfish or hake.

Crudités with walnut sauce

This sauce is delicious served with crudités, on bread and with pasta (like a Middle Eastern pesto). It is also particularly good stirred into baba ganoush (see page 159).

Chicken pieces with tarragon cream

Cook the chicken pieces as above. While they are resting, drain off most of the fat from the pan and add 200ml dry white wine or vermouth, if you have it. Add a splash of sherry vinegar and simmer to reduce, about 5 minutes. Pour 100ml double cream into the pan, and put back the chicken with 2 heaped tablespoons chopped fresh tarragon. Coat the chicken with the cream and serve with crusty bread and some spinach. Feeds 4.

NUT

Poached smoked haddock with walnut sauce

Sweat 2 sliced onions in 1 tablespoon butter for 10 minutes until soft. Lay the onion on a large piece of foil set in a baking dish. Place 3 or 4 smoked haddock fillets on top of the onion, and drizzle over 100ml chicken stock and 100ml white wine. Spread the walnut paste on top and wrap everything up in the foil. Bake in a preheated oven at 220°C/425°F/Gas Mark 7 for 10–15 minutes until the fish flakes apart easily. Feeds 4.

CASE

Duck confit with grape, walnut and roasted parsnip salad

This is a beautiful recipe to prepare one day when you have 10 minutes to spare and want to prepare something delicious for a rainy day. If you have already cooked the duck breast recipe on pages 110–11, you may already have some legs either fresh or in the deep-freeze (do make sure they are completely defrosted before starting the recipe) or you can buy some at the butcher's. Once the legs are salted, they can sit for 12–24 hours marinating in the cure. They are poached in duck fat for a few hours in a low oven and, when they are cooked, they can be stored in a large kilner jar for several months in a cool place. Whip them out when you are feeling like perking yourself up. The salad doesn't take longer than 40 minutes to pull together and is truly delicious. The grapes cut through the richness of the duck, while the sweetness of the parsnip brings the whole salad together.

FEEDS 6–8

For the confit

6 large duck legs (thighs and drumsticks)

10 tablespoons rock salt

5 bay leaves, crumbled

6 juniper berries, smashed using a mortar and pestle

1–2 teaspoons black peppercorns, smashed using a mortar and pestle

5 or 6 sprigs of fresh thyme or 1 tablespoon dried

6 whole garlic cloves, flattened with a rolling pin or the flat of a knife

1.5kg duck fat

For the salad

3 tablespoons duck fat (from the confit)

5 large parsnips, cut into slender wedges

80g walnuts

2 large shallots, finely sliced

Preheat the oven to 150°C/300°F/Gas Mark 2. Trim the duck legs of any excess fat and set this aside with the rest of the duck fat.

Mix together the salt, bay leaves, juniper berries, peppercorns, thyme and garlic, and rub all over the duck. Marinate in the refrigerator for 12–24 hours – any longer and the duck flesh can become quite salty.

When you are ready to cook the duck, melt the fat in a large, heavy-bottomed casserole dish or baking tray over a medium heat. Brush the salt off the duck legs and rinse in water, reserving the herbs and juniper berries for cooking the duck. Pat the legs dry and slip them into the fat in a single layer with the reserved seasonings. They should be covered in the fat; if you don't quite have enough, turn them from time to time during the cooking. Bring up to simmering point, then transfer to the oven and cook for 1½–2 hours until the meat is extremely soft. Carefully transfer the legs to a kilner jar or earthenware pot, and cover in the melted fat. They need to have at least 2.5cm of fat covering them. Store for up to 6 months in a cool larder or the refrigerator.

1 quantity of walnut oil dressing (see page 174)

4 baby gem lettuces, torn into shreds

200g red seedless grapes, halved

For the salad

Preheat the oven to 230°C/450°F/Gas Mark 8.

Heat the duck fat from the confit in a baking tray. Parboil the parsnips in salted, boiling water for 8–10 minutes. Drain and toss in the fat, and roast until crispy and caramelised, about 25–30 minutes. Meanwhile, toast the walnuts in the same oven, about 5 minutes, watching them like a hawk so that they don't burn.

Steep the shallot in the walnut oil dressing. Extract the duck legs from the kilner jar and wipe off any excess fat. Place the legs skin side down in a large baking tray. Roast in the oven for 10 minutes, then take out and pour any excess fat back into the jar (be careful – the fat will be extremely hot). Turn the legs over and roast for another 10 minutes until crispy and golden brown. The flesh should be falling off the legs.

Toss the parsnip, baby gem, walnuts and grapes in the walnut dressing. Scatter the salad with the falling-apart duck meat and serve.

Duck confit with green beans and shallots

Follow the recipe for preparing duck confit above. Steam 500g green beans until al dente, about 6–8 minutes. Toss in a sherry vinegar/shallot dressing (see page 174) with 150g sautéed mushrooms (page 60). Serve with boiled waxy potatoes.

Duck confit with blood orange and watercress salad

A blood orange and watercress or chicory salad will go beautifully with the confit, too, or the oranges can be substituted for the grapes in the master recipe. Blood oranges are in season from late January to mid March.

Wafer-thin pan-fried duck breast with tarragon and star anise

I had never cooked duck breast before *Masterchef*, where I realised how simple and delicious it was. It has an entirely different flavour to wild duck and is as easy to cook as a chicken breast. Making the marinade takes 5 minutes and, after a few hours marinating time, will tenderise the meat and allow it to take in all the flavours of the star anise and saba. This recipe is fast, sophisticated and unusual, which makes it perfect for a dinner party. A bit of home-made stock will enhance the marinade juices to make the incredibly good sauce. It goes well with the bagna cauda salad on page 185, a salad that is as delicious in winter as it is in summer. Do have potatoes as well if you like, but I'm not sure you need them.

FEEDS 4

2 large duck breasts, about 250g each

a little olive oil

1 tablespoon flour

1 heaped teaspoon redcurrant jelly or, better still, quince jelly if you can find it

dash of red wine (optional)

50ml chicken stock (see page 34) (optional)

For the marinade

generous handful of chopped fresh tarragon

50ml saba (see note on page 167) or 1 teaspoon treacle

juice of 1 lime

2 star anise, ground using a mortar and pestle

1–2 tablespoons olive oil

sea salt and freshly ground black pepper

Score the duck skin in a crisscross pattern, taking care not to cut into the meat. Mix all the marinade ingredients together. Put the breasts in the marinade mixture for a minimum of 1 hour (but preferably 3 or 4).

When you are ready to cook, heat the oven to its hottest possible setting, with a baking sheet inside. Next heat a thin coating of oil in a frying pan until smoking hot. Add the duck breasts (saving the marinade juices), skin side down, and pan-fry for 3–4 minutes, not worrying about the skin going black (this is from the sugar in the saba). Turn and seal the flesh on the underside for a minute, then place both breasts skin side up on your heated baking sheet. Cook for a further 4 minutes in the oven. Take out and leave to rest in a warm place by your hob for 5 minutes, spooning the fat on the baking sheet over the duck skin to keep the skin crisp. The breasts should still feel a little soft in the middle; the meat will carry on cooking as it rests. The resting time will tenderise the meat and finish off the cooking to leave the duck succulent and juicy, allowing the perfect amount of time for making the sauce.

To make the sauce, pour out most of the fat from the frying pan and put over a high heat, adding the flour. Scrape the flour around the pan for 2–3 minutes to cook it off, then add the reserved marinade juices a little at a time, stirring vigorously between additions to avoid lumps. Add the jelly, season with salt and pepper (and the red wine and stock, if you like), and let it bubble for a minute or two while you carve the duck, as thin as you can, diagonally across the width. Serve the wafer-thin slices of duck on warm plates with the juices poured over the top. Food fit for a king.

Winter salad of duck, blood oranges and toasted hazelnuts

I adore this for a smart winter salad. Add the duck to rocket, watercress or other bitter winter salad leaves such as trevisse, chicory or dandelion. Add 2–3 sliced blood oranges, 2 thinly shaved fennel bulbs and 80g roughly chopped toasted hazelnuts. Toss the salad in a light walnut oil dressing (see page 174) and serve. This salad is also glorious if you switch the duck breast for the duck confit on pages 106–7.

Blood oranges

Blood oranges are in season between January and February. They are beautiful when used in cooking and have a lovely sharp flavour, but more usual good-quality oranges will be just as good when blood oranges are unavailable. If you do get hold of some, try them freshly squeezed in champagne, or use them in the rhubarb and custard recipe on page 194.

Guinea fowl with lemon and caramelised garlic

This is an adaptation from a recipe in Colman Andrews's *Catalan Cuisine*, which is one of the most exciting cookbooks I have read. The area around Barcelona is an intriguing melting pot of flavours from around the world and it has long been my ambition to work there. This recipe is very simple and easy, but the flavours meld together to create a really good supper dish. Serve with garlic toast (see page 22) or plain boiled potatoes to soak up all the delicious juice, followed by a light green salad. I think this dish goes really well with the courgettes on page 154, too.

FEEDS 4

1 large guinea fowl or chicken, cut into 8 serving pieces

5 tablespoons olive oil

120g Serrano or other cured ham, sliced very finely into matchsticks

2 heads of garlic, separated and peeled

1 onion, chopped

3 sprigs of fresh thyme

½ teaspoon pimentón dulce (sweet smoked paprika)

600ml chicken stock (see page 34)

juice and zest of 1 lemon

juice of 1 orange

250ml dry white wine

sea salt and freshly ground black pepper

4 slices caramelised lemon (see below) or fresh lemon wedges to serve

Season the guinea fowl pieces all over with generous amounts of salt and pepper. Heat 4 tablespoons of the olive oil in a large casserole pan over a high heat and sauté the guinea fowl pieces, 4 at a time, until golden brown all over with crisp skin.

Remove the guinea fowl and add the remaining 1 tablespoon olive oil. Throw in the ham, whole garlic cloves and onion, and sauté until the onion has softened and the garlic cloves are turning a golden colour. Add the thyme, paprika, chicken stock, lemon zest and juice, orange juice and white wine, together with the guinea fowl, and bring to a simmer, tasting for seasoning. Simmer for 15 minutes, then remove the meat pieces with a slotted spoon and rest on the side. Simmer and reduce your sauce for another 20 minutes until it is rich-looking and syrupy.

Just before serving, return the meat pieces to the pan to warm through. Serve the guinea fowl with the caramelised lemon slices.

Caramelised lemon slices Cut a lemon into thick (6–7mm) slices. Melt 1 tablespoon butter in a frying pan over a medium-high heat and add the lemon. Sprinkle with a little salt and pepper, and a pinch of brown sugar, and cook until the slices are brown and caramelised on both sides, about 5 minutes.

Pot-roast pheasant with coconut and warm spices

Many people seem to be afraid of cooking pheasant and yet it is simple, delicious and good value for money. If you buy a brace at the butcher's, he can joint the pheasant for you or you can find out about local game dealers who now sell direct and deliver to all large cities. You can enjoy game for a limited season and be happy that they have led natural lives. This casserole takes 25 minutes to prepare at the most, and can be cooked well in advance. It emerges from the oven smelling warm and exotic – it is exceedingly good, with the coconut milk and spices giving it the subtlest hint of warmer climes.

FEEDS 6–8

3–4 tablespoons olive oil

2 pheasant, each jointed in 4 pieces

12 rashers unsmoked streaky bacon, chopped

10 shallots, finely sliced

3 garlic cloves, chopped

2 tablespoons spice mix (see page 85)

4 star anise, ground

10 prunes, pitted and roughly chopped

10 apricots, roughly chopped

300ml coconut milk (skimming off the top purée and discarding the water)

100ml brandy

chopped zest of 1 orange

2 bay leaves

600ml chicken stock

sea salt and freshly ground black pepper

Preheat the oven to 90°C/195°F/lowest possible gas setting.

In a large heatproof casserole dish, heat 2-3 tablespoons olive oil over a high heat and brown the pheasant joints on all sides for 5–10 minutes. Remove the pheasant and add the bacon, stirring to brown. When the bacon is cooked, set aside with the pheasant and pour another tablespoon of oil into the casserole dish. Throw in the shallot and sweat for 5 minutes before adding the garlic, spice mix and star anise. Season with salt and pepper.

Add the rest of the ingredients, including the pheasant and bacon, to the casserole. Bring to a simmer and cook in the oven for 3 hours. At this point you can remove the dish from the oven and let it sit in the refrigerator overnight, which will bring out all the flavours. You can even keep it in the fridge for a couple of days if you are pushed.

When you are ready to eat, heat the oven to 90°C/195°F/lowest possible gas setting. Bring the pot roast back to a simmer on the stove, transfer to the oven and cook for 1 hour more. Eat in shallow bowls, if you have them, with plenty of rice, couscous or quinoa to soak up all the juices.

Roast partridge with apricots, thyme and mascarpone

Game birds are so underrated. Nowadays you can go to a butcher and get partridge for a very reasonable sum. They are such small birds that I think they look lovely cut in half down the middle, with each half laid down on individual plates. Their subtle flavour is much less gamey than pheasant and they roast really well. If you can't get hold of partridge, you can use wood pigeon. This recipe is magic. The stuffing melts inside the bird and the bread sits underneath, absorbing all the flavours and juices of the meat and stuffing. Alternatively, roast extra bread in the pan with the juices and make a partridge bread salad with lots of raw baby spinach, watercress and a few capers.

FEEDS 4

3 large slices of bread

75g butter

2 large partridge,

125g thinly cut streaky bacon

For the stuffing

180g mascarpone

180g cottage cheese

180g mix of sultanas, raisins and chopped dried apricots

2 heaped tablespoons chopped fresh marjoram

2 heaped tablespoons chopped fresh thyme leaves

sea salt and freshly ground black pepper

Preheat the oven to 220°C/425°F/Gas Mark 7.

Cut the crusts off the bread and generously butter each side. Cut each slice in half and arrange in two lines in a baking tray.

Season the partridge inside and out with salt and pepper. Mix the stuffing ingredients together and push inside the birds. Place each bird on top of 3 slices of bread, and cover with butter and slices of streaky bacon. Roast for 10 minutes, then remove the bacon, basting the birds with the pan juices (do this with the tray out of the oven and the oven door shut to keep the oven hot). Continue roasting for another 5 minutes before reducing the oven temperature to 170°C/340°F/Gas Mark 3-4. Roast for another 15–20 minutes, then remove from the oven and rest, covered with foil, for at least 10 minutes. This is delicious served with breadcrumbs fried in garlic and butter until crisp and toasted, and heaps of spinach (see page 157).

Note It is traditional in Britain to roast game birds fast in very hot ovens. Another way you can cook a partridge is for 45 minutes at a lower temperature (180°C/350°F/Gas Mark 4). It is simply a matter of preference.

Partridge salad with walnuts

Try jointing the roast partridge into breasts, legs and thighs. Dress watercress with walnut oil and toasted walnuts, and toss through the partridge and stuffing.

Fish and seafood

Fish are slippery suckers. They have an enviable reputation for being slimming, good for you, full of useful oils, minerals and proteins. Yet I used to have an irrational fear of cooking them. Now that I have conquered that fear, I find that I was not alone. I talk to friends and they voice all the doubts and misgivings that I once had. It was only after having to cook so much fish on the set of *MasterChef* that I realised how foolish I had been. Fish is very easy to cook well, but all too easy to overcook. However, if you adhere to a few basic principles, you will find success and can wow all your friends, lovers and colleagues. Fish loves to be cooked fast, above all else. And fast cooking means fast food. So fish is, in fact, the ultimate fast food.

Unless you are poaching a piece of fish, or gently simmering some in a delicious fish stew, always go by the strict principle (that is also true of most meat) that fish love to be grilled, fried or baked in very, very high heat. So whether you are pan-frying a nice bit of tuna or halibut, sautéing some king prawns or char-grilling some delicious, plump scallops, do make sure that your frying pan is smoking hot before you even think of adding a slosh of olive oil or a knob of butter. Once it has started smoking, add your fat, letting it really heat up and sizzle – then slap on your fish. This way you develop a lovely brown crust to your fish as the flesh begins to cook. If you are cooking fish fillets or steaks, you can then leave them in the pan for 4–5 minutes, totally untouched and sizzling at the highest possible heat. Then just pop them into an equally hot oven (the hotter, the better) in the same pan, if possible, and finish off the cooking there. A 200g piece of fish shouldn't take more than 4–5 minutes more and will just lose its translucency when it is cooked. The flesh will flake off easily.You can tell when it is starting to overcook because the flesh starts going rubbery and oozing a whiteish goo from the sides. Always err on the side of undercooking – if you have to throw it back in the oven for a few minutes, no harm is done. If you overcook a bit of fish, however, it totally ruins the pleasure of biting into the soft, delicate flesh.

A cautionary tale

I find it impossible to write about the joy of fish and the pleasure of eating it without also mentioning how little time we will have left to eat it, if we continue to exploit it as we do currently. **We will not have unfarmed fish left in the sea in 15–20 years at the rate we are depleting the seas' stocks at present.** That would appear to be an incontrovertible fact (do read Charles Clover's remarkable book *The End of the Line* if you don't believe me).

When buying fish, do ask your fishmonger where the fish has come from and if it is fished in a sustainable way (line-caught is good). If you are in doubt and care about these things, log on to www.fishonline.org, the Marine Conservation Society's brilliant website, which tells you fish to eat and fish to avoid.

Pan-fried fillet of halibut with spicy chickpeas and chorizo

This was inspired by a trip to the Anglesea, my all-time favourite pub, which constantly has me rushing back to my kitchen to try to adapt their recipes for home cooking. They served this as a starter with balls of tender deep-fried skate cheek in beer batter, with the smoothest chickpea sauce drizzled over the top and chunks of juicy chorizo sausage on the side. This version is much, much easier to cook at home, but I hope you agree tastes pretty good. The slightly curried hummus is a heavenly combination with the tender, juicy fish.

SERVES 6-8

2 x 400g tins cooked chickpeas, drained, or 300g dried, soaked overnight and cooked (see page 151)

250ml chickpea cooking liquid or water or stock

4 tablespoons extra virgin olive oil, plus extra to serve (optional)

2 medium onions, chopped

3 garlic cloves, chopped

1 tablespoon spice mix (see page 85)

1 tablespoon good-quality red wine vinegar

180g cooking chorizo, chopped

2 tablespoons olive oil

6 halibut fillets, preferably Pacific, about 200g each, or 1.2 kg hake in pieces

2 tablespoons chopped fresh coriander

lemon wedges to serve

Preheat the oven to 200°C/400°F/Gas Mark 6.

Whizz the chickpeas in a food processor, slowly adding the cooking liquid to create a smooth mash. Heat 2 tablespoons of the extra virgin olive oil in a heatproof casserole over a medium heat and cook the onion for 7-8 minutes until it starts to soften. Add the garlic and spice mix, and cook for a further 2-3 minutes. Add the onion mix to the chickpeas and whizz some more with the remaining 2 tablespoons extra virgin olive oil and the vinegar. Put in a saucepan and heat gently, waiting for everything else.

Meanwhile, fry the chorizo in a frying pan, breaking up into small pieces with a wooden spoon (you almost want chorizo crumbs). In a large pan, heat the olive oil until sizzling hot and add the fish steaks. Fry without touching for 4-5 minutes to get a really good crispy coating. Put in the oven for another 3-4 minutes to finish the cooking.

Stir the coriander through the chickpeas and serve with the chorizo crumbled on top, a slab of fish on the side and a big wedge of lemon. Drizzle with extra virgin olive oil, if you like.

Note Fish such as this is also delicious with other pulses. Try some on a bed of saffron cannellini beans (page 151). When buying your halibut, bear in mind that is better to eat Pacific halibut, rather than Atlantic.

Mediterranean baked fish

This dish was inspired by a chef I met when I was waitressing in Chile. One weekend the chef, originally a fisherman by trade, took us all back to his fishing village four hours down the coast and showed us what a real fish stew was. It was cooked in a vast oil drum, with the potatoes on the bottom, then the green vegetables and, lastly, the fish and seafood at the top. It was the best thing I had ever tasted and fed the whole village. Like our British fish pie, it is both warming and comforting. Instead of a mash crust, the potatoes are sliced and cooked in the pie, melting into all the delicious olive oil and garlic flavours. I've used gurnard in this, but it is also delicious with halibut, sea bass, hake or monkfish (but take care to cook the monkfish for a little longer).

SERVES 6

1kg mixture of gurnard, sea bass, red mullet or monkfish, filleted

4 tablespoons plain flour, seasoned with sea salt and freshly ground black pepper

about 120ml extra virgin olive oil

4 sprigs of fresh curly parsley, finely chopped, plus extra to serve

4 garlic cloves, finely chopped

150ml good-quality cooking brandy

1 slice country-style bread

12 almonds, blanched and toasted

1 medium onion, chopped

4 tomatoes, peeled, seeded and chopped (see tip on page 136 for peeling tomatoes), or 1 x 400g tin peeled plum tomatoes, chopped

2 celery sticks, chopped

large pinch of pimentón (smoked paprika)

850g potatoes, peeled and cut into 1cm slices

600ml fish stock or mixture of water and wine

2 sprigs of fresh thyme

3 bay leaves

sea salt and freshly ground black pepper

Cut the fish into bite-size chunks and toss in the seasoned flour. Heat 2 tablespoons of the oil in a large heatproof casserole and, when it is smoking hot, add one-third of the fish. Fry in batches for a couple of minutes a side until golden brown, removing the fish between batches and using more oil if needed (it is important not to crowd the fish so that it gets a lovely crust and doesn't stew).

Put all the fish back in the pan (still over a high heat) and sprinkle with half the parsley and half the garlic. Pour over the brandy and ignite (be careful!). When the flames have died down, transfer to a bowl. Heat 1 tablespoon of the oil in the same pan and fry the bread for the picada (see note) on both sides until golden, then grind up with the nuts and the remaining garlic. Set aside.

Sauté the onion for 7–8 minutes until soft. Add the tomato, celery and pimentón. Season with salt and pepper, and cook for another 7–8 minutes. Add the potato, stock, thyme and bay leaves. Simmer for 30 minutes until the potato is tender. Stir in the picada, put the fish back in the casserole and simmer for another few minutes. Check the seasoning and serve sprinkled with the extra parsley. Follow with a fresh green salad.

Note Picada is the Catalan name of a paste or roux usually made up of garlic, breadcrumbs and nuts, with which you can thicken and flavour soups and stews.

Variations

This is delicious with 1 fennel bulb, chopped and caramelised with the onion. For a more traditional bouillabaisse, add 1 teaspoon fennel seed, a pinch of saffron threads and 1 teaspoon crushed dried chilli, and serve with large crostini and saffron mayonnaise (see pages 16 and 69). Ancho chilli is also often used in this dish if you can get hold of it. Simply soak the dried ancho chilli, remove the stem and seeds, chop the flesh and add it when you are cooking the onion.

You can also omit the potato and simmer the stew for a few minutes to cook the fish in the broth and serve with Spanish saffron rice. Or just enjoy as a delicious fish and fennel broth with large chunks of sautéed fennel thrown in. Yum!

Tommi's tip

When buying tinned tomatoes, always choose whole peeled plum tomatoes – they are a much better quality than tins of ready-chopped tomatoes.

Pimentón

Pimentón is smoked paprika in powdered form. It is sold as pimentón dulce or pimentón picante, which are the sweet and hot varieties, respectively. Buy both and experiment with their flavours in fish stews, tomato sauces, soups and stews. Try a little sprinkled over croûtons or mixed with salt for a quail's egg dip. It is also delicious added to home-made mayonnaise. You should be able to find pimentón in good supermarkets, delicatessens and gourmet food shops.

Organic salmon balls with marjoram and saffron

This recipe is adapted from Alice Waters's mouthwatering *Chez Panisse Café* cookbook and is a truly sensational starter. The original recipe uses belly of tuna which, marbled with fat, is perfect for these balls. However, much as I love tuna (see the sashimi on page 28 for one of my favourite recipes), I try to avoid using it where I can as it is a fish fast heading for extinction. Here I have used organic farmed salmon instead, the flesh of which has the same fatty, meaty quality as tuna. Be sure to buy organic here, though, as the quality of non-organic farmed salmon is hopeless.

FEEDS 4–6

1 medium onion, finely diced

olive oil for frying

1½ tablespoons chopped fresh marjoram or thyme (if you can't get marjoram)

small pinch of saffron threads

pinch of chilli flakes

4 tablespoons raisins, soaked in hot water for 5 minutes

180g dried breadcrumbs (see page 156)

70–80ml milk

500g organic farmed salmon

4 tablespoons pine nuts, toasted and roughly chopped

½ teaspoon pimentón picante (hot smoked paprika)

1 egg, beaten

plain flour, seasoned with sea salt and pepper, for rolling

1 lemon, halved

extra virgin olive oil

rocket

sea salt and freshly ground black pepper

Sauté the onion in the oil for 5 minutes. Add the marjoram, saffron and chilli flakes, and sauté for a further 5 minutes until the onion is soft and transparent, but not coloured.

Drain the raisins and soak the breadcrumbs in the milk. Slice the salmon thinly, then cut the slices into strips. Cut the strips into small cubes that will hold together in your fish balls.

Mix the salmon, onion mixture, pine nuts, raisins and breadcrumbs in a bowl, and stir in the pimentón and beaten egg. Season with salt and pepper, and if you like a few more chilli flakes. At this stage, heat a little oil in a frying pan and fry a little ball of the mix to taste for seasoning.

Divide the mixture (which should be about 1kg) into 18 small balls, about 55g each, rolling them in some seasoned flour. Fry in a little olive oil over a medium heat for 2–3 minutes a side until nicely browned and cooked all the way through. Alternatively, for a quick fun supper, divide the mix into 6 fish cakes, roll in seasoned plain flour and fry until golden all over.

Serve the delicious balls on a bed of seasoned rocket drizzled with your best extra virgin olive oil, a squeeze of lemon juice and shaved pecorino or manchego cheese, with plenty of fresh, crusty bread. Or for a quick, delicious supper, make the mixture into fish cakes and serve with the rocket salad on the side and some basil and Parmesan quinoa (see page 148).

Slow-cooked sea trout with verjuice and sorrel beurre blanc

Maggie Beer introduced me to verjuice (see page 130) and taught me how to do this easy, pretty foolproof beurre blanc at one of her workshops. She adds cream to the beurre blanc to stabilise the sauce. Purists may be appalled, but why not make life easy? The sauce is subtle and rich, and a perfect foil for sea trout. If you are really lucky you may be able to get hold of wild salmon, but failing that you can substitute the sea trout with organic farmed salmon.

SERVES 4

1 sea trout, cleaned and scaled

3 or 4 white peppercorns

½ teaspoon fennel seed

2 bay leaves

2 or 3 sprigs of fresh parsley

1 onion, halved

sea salt

3–4 tablespoons finely grated lemon zest to serve

finely chopped fresh chives to serve

For the beurre blanc

250ml verjuice or 150ml white wine vinegar

6 shallots, finely sliced

1½ tablespoons double cream

350g unsalted butter, diced

squeeze of lemon juice

15g fresh sorrel, finely chopped

Put the sea trout in a fish kettle with the peppercorns, fennel seed, bay leaves, parsley and onion, and sprinkle with a little sea salt. Cover with water. Bring the water to a simmer and continue simmering for a few minutes before turning the heat off. Allow the fish to cool in the water, but test it after 20 minutes and then again at 30 minutes if necessary. The skin should flake off the bone easily when cooked. If the fish is cooked before the water cools, lift out of the water and set aside.

To make the beurre blanc, heat the verjuice and shallot, and simmer until it is reduced by two-thirds. The liquid should be rich and syrupy. Season with a little salt. Add the double cream, then gradually whisk in the butter, 2 or 3 lumps at a time, never letting the mixture boil or it will separate. When all the butter has been added and the sauce is thick, season with salt and pepper, and a squeeze of lemon juice. Stir in the sorrel and keep in a warm place.

When the trout is cooked, carefully remove the skin. Put on a large serving dish scattered with chopped chives and lemon zest. Serve in tranches (i.e. cut across the fillet at an angle), lifted off the bone, with the sorrel beurre blanc poured over the top and scattered with more chives and lemon zest, and accompanied by some baby new potatoes.

Variation

Maggie Beer also serves this sauce over scallops seared on a griddle, which makes a glorious starter.

Prawns al ajillo

I love this dish, which I first tried when I was working in Chile. It takes moments to cook and is really good. Here I have given starter quantities, but by all means up the amounts and serve for a summery lunch dish.

SERVES 4

6 tablespoons olive oil

4 garlic cloves, finely chopped

1 fresh red chilli, seeded and finely chopped, or 1 teaspoon pasilla chilli flakes

20 king prawns or 400g shrimp, peeled and deveined

3 tablespoons white wine

squeeze of lemon juice

2 tablespoons chopped fresh flat-leaf parsley

sea salt and freshly ground black pepper

Heat the oil in a large pan and, when it is hot, add the garlic and chilli. Cook for 1–2 minutes until the garlic is taking some colour (but not burning), then add the prawns. Cook for a few minutes until the prawns are just turning pink. Add the white wine and lemon juice, and bubble up for a moment or two. Season with salt and pepper, and scatter with the parsley. Serve at once.

This is delicious as a starter served with lots of fresh, crusty bread to mop up juices, but try it tossed through spaghetti for a very fast supper dish.

Five-minute flash-baked mackerel

Mackerel are amazing fish: inexpensive, extremely good for you and full of flavour (and due to their fast spawning they are a sound fish to choose for ethical shopping). Their rich flesh lends itself beautifully to different spices, too, so do try the different versions below. A friend, Robin, was an ardent mackerel-hater until he was converted by the lemon and cumin version which I first found in one of my favourite cookbooks, Sam and Sam Clarke's *Moro*. It is important that the mackerel are spankingly fresh, so I would advise getting them from a trusted fishmonger. They should smell of the sea, rather than fishy, and be bright and shiny.

SERVES 4

4 small fresh mackerel, gutted but otherwise left whole

extra virgin olive oil

2 lemons, halved

sea salt and freshly ground black pepper

Preheat the oven to 220°C/425°F/Gas Mark 7.

Season the fish inside and out with plenty of salt and pepper. Place on a baking tray and drizzle with a little extra virgin olive oil. Bake on the top shelf of the oven for 5 minutes or until the flesh comes away from the bone easily. Serve with the parsley and olive salad below, lemon halves and boiled new potatoes drizzled with more extra virgin olive oil and seasoned with salt and pepper. I also love them with boiled beetroot tossed in a French dressing (see page 174) while still warm and a dollop of fresh horseradish cream (page 16).

Parsley, tomato and olive salad

Combine 1 large bunch of roughly chopped fresh flat-leaf parsley leaves, 3 or 4 ripe plum tomatoes cut into 1–2cm dice, 50g roughly chopped finest-quality black olives and 2 tablespoons finely chopped red onion in a bowl. Add a good squeeze of lemon juice to taste and serve the salad with the mackerel fillets.

Mackerel with cumin, lemon and flat-leaf parsley

Fillet the mackerel and cook as above for 4 minutes. Scatter with 2 teaspoons ground cumin, a large handful of roughly chopped fresh parsley and 3 very finely chopped garlic cloves. Squeeze over some lemon juice and serve.

Madras-style mackerel

Make 3 or 4 diagonal slashes into each side of the gutted whole mackerel. Heat 90g coriander seed, 2 tablespoons cumin seed, 1 teaspoon black peppercorns, 1 teaspoon mustard seed, 1 teaspoon chilli powder and 1 teaspoon salt. Grind to a paste using a coffee grinder or mortar and pestle with 3 garlic cloves and a 2.5cm piece of peeled fresh ginger. Stir in 1 tablespoon cider vinegar and 3 tablespoons groundnut, vegetable or olive oil. Stuff the paste into the mackerel slashes and bake in a preheated 220°C/425°F/Gas Mark 7 oven for 3–4 minutes on each side. Serve with green coriander rice (see page 148).

Note Try cooking mackerel on a char-grill – a delicious way to eat mackerel or fresh sardines, guts and all, drizzled with olive oil and served with a black olive and tomato relish or the salsa verde on page 72.

Mackerel brandade

SERVES 6–8

3 mackerel, gutted but otherwise left whole

3 medium potatoes, about 300g, peeled and chopped

200ml extra virgin olive oil plus extra for baking and drizzling

200ml milk

3 garlic cloves, peeled and crushed

juice of 1 lemon

100g chopped black olives (or try garlic or anchovy-stuffed green olives)

handful of roughly chopped fresh flat-leaf parsley

sea salt and freshly ground black pepper

Preheat the oven to 220°C/425°F/Gas Mark 7.

Cook the mackerel as in the main flash-baked mackerel recipe at left, taking the flesh off the bone once the fish have baked for 5 minutes in the oven. Boil the potato in water until soft, then mash. In two separate pans, gently heat the 200ml extra virgin olive oil and the milk, into which you have thrown the crushed garlic. Put the mash in the food processor with the fish and slowly add the milk (including the poached garlic), heated oil and lemon juice. Season with salt and pepper.

Serve in a beautiful shallow bowl, drizzled with more extra virgin olive oil, the black olives and the parsley. This is delicious on toast, or with crudités. Put fennel, organic carrots (for flavour), celery, red peppers, radishes, boiled artichoke hearts on another plate, and place both plates on the table for a starter or a lovely, light lunch with some fresh bread and cheese or fruit to follow.

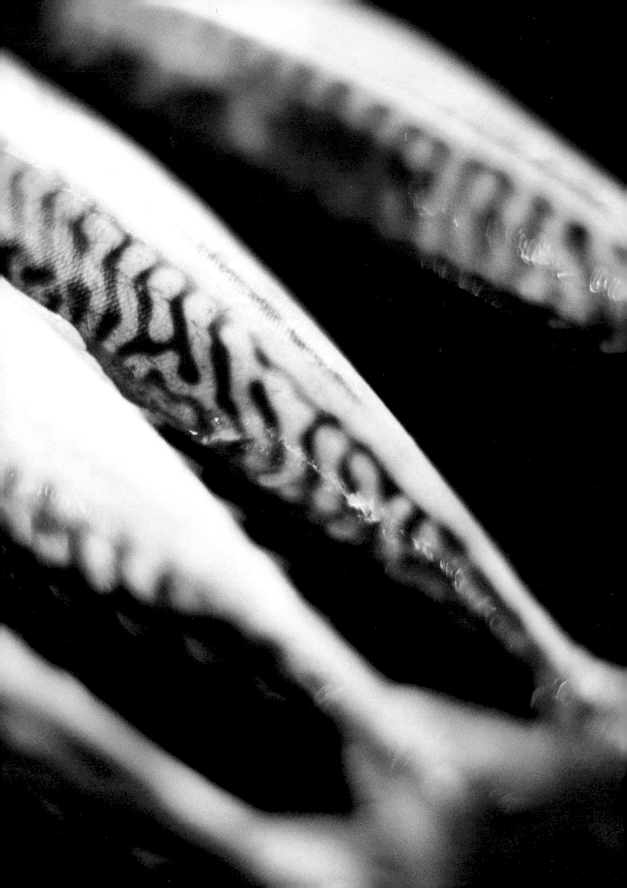

Sardines escabeche

Sardines are a wonder food. They are extremely cheap and incredibly good for you as they are full of omega-3 oils, classic brain food. This recipe is great as it is dead easy, takes only 20 minutes and can be eaten as a starter or tossed in spaghettini for a delicious pasta dish. The best thing is that, once the sardines are flash-fried, you can leave them to marinate in the onion dressing overnight or during the day, meaning you are cutting down on any last-minute work.

SERVES 4

4 tablespoons olive oil

2 red onions, finely sliced

3 bay leaves

2 sprigs of fresh thyme

3 garlic cloves, sliced

4 tablespoons verjuice (see note) or white wine vinegar

3 tablespoons raisins

8–12 fresh sardines, gutted and filleted

a little flour, seasoned with sea salt and black pepper

juice and zest of 1 lemon

3 tablespoons pine nuts, toasted

small handful of fresh flat-leaf parsley, roughly chopped

sea salt and freshly ground black pepper

Heat 2 tablespoons of the olive oil in a heavy saucepan over a medium heat and add the onion, bay leaves and thyme. Sweat in the oil for 5 minutes, then add the garlic. Sweat for another 7–8 minutes until the onion is translucent. Meanwhile, warm the verjuice in a small pan with 50ml water. Add the raisins and soak for 5–10 minutes to plump them up. Add the raisins and juices to the onion mixture.

Dust the sardine fillets in seasoned flour. Heat the remaining 2 tablespoons oil in a heavy frying pan over a high heat. Fry the sardine fillets in batches until golden brown, about 40 seconds a side. Transfer the sardines to a plate and pour over the onion marinade and its juices. Squeeze over some lemon juice. Scatter with the pine nuts, parsley and the lemon zest. Leave the flavours to marinate for a minimum of 30 minutes. Serve at room temperature.

Spaghettini with sardines and pine nuts

Follow the recipe above for the sardines. Cook 500g spaghettini until al dente and toss it with 1 tablespoon extra virgin olive oil and the marinated sardines. Scatter with toasted breadcrumbs (see page 156) and serve for a cheap but fast supper dish.

Verjuice

Verjuice is the juice of unripe grapes and has a lovely tangy, fresh flavour. It can be used as a softer, subtler alternative to vinegar in salad dressings, hollandaise and other sauces. It is just starting to be imported into the United Kingdom. Ask for it at your local deli or look for it through online suppliers.

Pan-fried scallops with summer herb salsa

Scallops are at their best when cooked really fast over a high heat. Pan-frying does this to perfection, caramelising and blackening the slightly sweet flesh on the outside, allowing the inside to stay as soft as butter. There are three recipes for scallops here, all using this cooking method. The first light, zingy Thai version is perfect for a sophisticated lunch or supper. Omit the rice for a light lunch or a starter. The second is another salad, as good in winter as in summer, with a subtly smoked cream sauce which is complemented by the sweet scallop flavour and the zing of the capers. The third recipe is a favourite of mine, combining gutsy black pudding with bacon and the blackened scallops. For all three, do make sure you use a heavy pan that is smoking hot before you add the oil. For a feast, serve 5 scallops per person instead of 3.

SERVES 6

250g Thai rice, rinsed

2 tablespoons sesame oil

1 tablespoon rice wine vinegar

mixed salad leaves (rocket, chicory, red, watercress, baby gem lettuce)

1 small bunch each of fresh coriander, fresh mint and fresh basil leaves

18 scallops

3 tablespoons extra virgin olive oil

sea salt and freshly ground black pepper

For the summer herb salsa

large bunch of fresh mint, chopped

large bunch of fresh coriander, chopped

3 spring onions, chopped, or 3 tablespoons chopped fresh chives

2 teaspoons honey

2 fresh green chillies

1 garlic clove

2 tablespoons rice wine vinegar

juice of 2 limes

120ml extra virgin olive oil

Cook the rice in boiling, salted water for 10 minutes. Drain, stir in the sesame oil and wine vinegar, season with salt and pepper, and set aside to cool.

Meanwhile, whizz the salsa herbs, spring onion, honey, chillies, garlic, rice wine vinegar and lime juice in a food processor. Add the extra virgin olive oil, season with plenty of salt and pepper, and process to a fairly smooth dressing. Stir into the rice (or reserve, if you are not using the rice).

Divide the salad leaves among 6 serving plates. Scatter with the basil, coriander and mint leaves.

Season the scallops with salt and pepper. Heat the 3 tablespoons olive oil in a large frying pan until smoking hot and add the scallops in 2 or 3 batches (if you add too many you will lower the heat in the pan and stop the scallops from frying). Fry for 1–2 minutes on each side until they have a golden, almost burnt skin. When you have cooked each batch, transfer the scallops to the cooling rice (toss the scallops and salad leaves in the reserved dressing if you are leaving the rice out). Serve with 3 scallops on each pile of salad leaves.

Scallop salad with capers and smoked anchovy cream

Heat 2 tablespoons butter in a small saucepan over a low heat. Add 8 anchovy fillets and cook for 5 minutes, breaking up the anchovies with a wooden spoon and 'melting' them into the butter. Add 300ml double cream and the juice of 1 lemon, and warm through. Cook the scallops as above and serve them on a bed of bitter salad leaves with a scattering of small capers and drizzled with the smoked anchovy cream.

Pan-fried scallops with black pudding, bacon and rocket

For a more wintry dish, fry 200g sliced black pudding in a little olive oil with 6–8 rashers of chopped bacon. Pan-fry the scallops as above. Serve the black pudding, bacon and scallops on a bed of rocket with plenty of freshly squeezed lemon juice and crusty bread for a starter. Serve them with the lentils on page 150 for a glamorous supper dish.

Pasta, grains and pulses

Pulses and grains – the sort of food that vegans and hippies were known to eat. Their carbohydrate-rich qualities were derided by the figure-conscious and protein-dieters. Happily, we are coming out of those dark ages and people have embraced these wonder foods for all they offer. To start with there is so much variety: cannellini beans, borlotti beans, butter beans, black-eye beans, red kidney beans, green lentils, split lentils, brown lentils, Puy lentils, pearl barley, bulgur, white rice, brown rice, wild rice, red camargue rice, arborio rice, Thai rice, Japanese sticky rice. The choice is endless, as is the repertoire of easy, imaginative recipes that you can cook. These foodstuffs are also rich in protein and extremely good for the digestive system. Talk to any nutritionist and they will tell you about the anti-carcinogenic properties of pulses and grains. They are also cheap and easy to store.

On an entirely different note, think about these pulses and grains in terms of flavour. What would life be like without the occasional supper of smooth cannellini beans or a rich, comforting polenta or soupy lentils spiked with lardons of bacon and wild mushrooms? My favourite easy supper is a plate of beans doused in masses of olive oil and garlic with whatever is lying in my cupboard or fridge, be it tuna, chicken or a simple salad. Quinoa is the new supergrain that is becoming really popular. It is packed with goodness and, like couscous, absorbs other flavours readily. It is dead easy to cook and delicious drizzled with basil oil and served with masses of grated Parmesan. Get creative and try it with some of the sauces on pages 68–76 to ring the changes (it's great with salsa romesco and stir-fried shrimp).

Pasta is another thing altogether. A great supper dish, it can be thrown together with a tin of tomatoes and a bit of chilli, or be oozing with a pine nut, hazelnut or walnut pesto. Embellish it with a seasonal vegetable or sandwich it around a slow-cooked Italian-style ragu. There are very few people who are not seduced by a big bowl of steaming pasta. And pasta options are not limited to the recipes in this chapter alone, as you will find many of my other recipes can be turned into pasta dishes very successfully. These include:

- Joe's tuna delight with borlotti beans, chilli and extra virgin olive oil (page 61)
- Prawns al ajillo (page 125)
- Sardines escabeche (page 130)
- Sicilian broccoli pesto (page 158)
- Char-grilled courgette wedges with basil, mint, chilli and lemon (page 154)
- Roast aubergine with pomegranate, feta and mint (page 160)
- Curly kale with olive oil and garlic (page 164)
- Char-grilled winter vegetables with blue cheese (page 179)
- Broad bean salad with mint, lemon zest and goat's cheese (page 187)

Thirty-minute fusilli

This light summery pasta dish is perfect for al fresco eating with a bottle of chilled white wine. If you can, make the breadcrumbs from a stale but good-quality sourdough or country loaf – the flavour will be much better. Visit a market towards the end of the summer or late at weekends and you will be able to buy mounds of sweet, ripe tomatoes at great discounts.

FEEDS 6

500g fusilli pasta

4 tablespoons extra virgin olive oil

250g stale bread, coarsely crumbed in a food processor (see page 156)

25g butter

2 garlic cloves, crushed

4 tablespoons mixed fresh summer herbs (thyme, basil, mint, marjoram, parsley, chervil)

500g very ripe tomatoes, skinned, seeded and diced into small cubes (see tip)

pinch of soft brown sugar

sea salt and freshly ground black pepper

Put the pasta into a large saucepan with plenty of boiling water, salt and a good tablespoon of olive oil. Fry the breadcrumbs in the butter and 2 tablespoons of the olive oil. When turning a nice golden brown, add the garlic and continue to cook for another 5 minutes. Set aside. (Alternatively, toast the breadcrumbs in the oil in a hot oven, spread out on a baking tray.) When the pasta is just cooked (still with a bite to it), drain and toss with the herbs, breadcrumbs, tomato and remaining olive oil. Add the sugar and season with salt and pepper. Serve at once.

Thirty-minute fusilli with Serrano ham and manchego cheese

Make the recipe as above, but toss with about 100g each of shredded Serrano ham and diced manchego cheese.

Tommi's tip

Skinning tomatoes is fast and easy. Boil a kettle and pour the boiling water over the tomatoes to cover them. Let them sit in the hot water for 20–30 seconds (counting aloud helps), until the skins starts peeling off when you prick a tomato with a sharp knife. Drain immediately and peel. My mother likes to squeeze the peelings over the tomatoes, as she insists that the juice that comes out has the best flavour.

Angel hair pasta with clams, prawns and thyme

This is a delicious recipe of my mother's which I refused to cook for years because I foolishly couldn't believe that anything that was so easy to make could taste so sophisticated and good. How wrong I was.

   It takes about 15 minutes to cook from start to finish. Perfect if you have a few friends for supper, but have run out of time. Just nip out in your lunch hour for the shellfish and cream, and relax. You can cook it with any seafood – cockles, squid, tiger prawns, scallops – so play around. The cooking method is very similar to vongole, the classic meld of clams, garlic, chilli, white wine and parsley (see below), but also works very well with the Thai flavours in another variation. Yet more proof that fast food needn't be bad for you.

Note Do check that none of your friends is allergic to shellfish, so that you aren't concocting something else at the last minute.

FEEDS 4

4 tablespoons olive oil

5 shallots, finely chopped

3 fresh thyme sprigs

½ garlic clove, crushed

1kg of seafood (mix of cockles, clams, prawns and mussels)

240ml fruity white wine, warmed gently

350g angel hair pasta or spaghettini

1 tablespoon oyster sauce

½ teaspoon anchovy essence

240ml double cream

good handful of chopped fresh flat-leaf parsley

sea salt and freshly ground black pepper

You will need 2 very large pans to make this dish. Put a large saucepan of salted water on to boil, and make sure that you have pasta plates warming in your oven at the lowest possible setting, or just microwave them 5 minutes before you are ready to serve. Heat the olive oil in a pan over a medium heat. Sweat the shallot and thyme gently and, when the shallot is turning translucent, add the garlic.

   When you are quite sure that you can get everyone sitting at the table in 10 minutes, start the rest of the recipe – there is nothing as unappetising as cold seafood pasta.

   Add the seafood and half the wine to the shallot mixture, and warm through very gently, without simmering – otherwise the seafood will become rubbery. Drop the pasta into the pan of simmering water. It won't take more than 3–4 minutes to cook it to al dente. Add the rest of the wine, the oyster sauce and the anchovy essence to the seafood. Fish out the thyme stalks and stir in the cream. Bring to just below simmering point and cook for a few more minutes until the mussels, clams and cockles have opened up and the prawns have turned from translucent to pink. It is important not to overcook the seafood so that it stays soft and tender, not rubbery and chewy.

Toss the cooked pasta with the seafood sauce, and scatter with the parsley and serve on piping-hot plates with a crisp green salad to follow.

Pasta alle vongole

Finely grate 2 cloves garlic into 2 tablespoons olive oil. Stir in 2 seeded and finely chopped medium fresh red chillies. Heat a large saucepan until smoking and add the garlic/chilli mixture and 750g cleaned clams. Toss the clams in the mixture for 1–2 minutes, then add 500ml warmed dry white wine. Shake the clams in the wine and cook, covered, for 5 minutes or until all the clams have opened. (Discard any that do not open.) In the meantime, cook 350g angel hair pasta until al dente, 3–4 minutes. Serve the clam sauce with the angel hair pasta and a good handful of chopped fresh flat-leaf parsley.

Angel hair pasta with smoked oysters

For real emergencies – but nonetheless delicious – you can substitute the seafood with tinned smoked oysters, but do go easy on the salt.

Angel hair pasta with Thai prawns, ginger, chilli and coconut

Stir-fry 3 chopped shallots and 2 garlic cloves in 2 tablespoons vegetable oil over a high heat. After a minute, add a 25cm piece fresh ginger, 1 lemongrass stalk and 1 fresh green chilli, all finely chopped. After 2 minutes, add a lime leaf and 4 celery sticks cut into thin lengths. Throw in a large handful of beansprouts, some chopped water chestnuts and a mixture of 1kg of seafood (as above). Stir-fry for 2–3 minutes before adding 200ml coconut milk and the juice of 2 limes. Serve tossed with angel hair pasta (see above), sprinkled with chopped fresh coriander leaves and seasoned with a good shake of fish sauce.

Lizzie's pasta

This pasta dish is similar to the hazelnut and preserved lemon pesto I make (see page 70), but it uses the seeds from butternut squash instead of hazelnuts. It is delicious. The recipe belongs to a great girl, Liz Stretch, whom I met in Borough Market and with whom I have spent many cosy evenings, enjoying and talking about good food. She is a great cook and makes a mean Bakewell tart!

FEEDS 4

2 medium butternut squash (with seeds), about 800g each

a little olive oil

2 garlic cloves, finely chopped

1 large fresh red chilli, seeded and chopped

1 large bunch of fresh mint, chopped

good-quality extra virgin olive oil

Parmesan, freshly grated

300g pappardelle or any other pasta with a large flat surface area (farfalle, the butterflies, are also good)

Maldon sea salt

Preheat the oven to 200°C/400°F/Gas Mark 6.

Peel the squash and carefully remove all the seeds, taking off all of the stringy pieces of the squash that attach to the seeds. Pat the seeds dry with absorbent kitchen paper. Cut the squash into smallish chunks, place in a tray and pour in some olive oil and sea salt. Roast for 30-40 minutes.

Either grill or fry (in a little olive oil) the seeds on a very low heat until golden but not too brown. They should be cooked through just enough to crush finely into your pesto. Watch out for the popping seeds that fly out of the pan if you are frying! You don't want to lose any, as these are crucial to the pesto's unique flavour.

Crush the seeds using a mortar and pestle. Add the garlic, chilli and mint, and crush together to get a lovely texture. Alternatively, blend in a food processor with the seeds (although food processors tend to overmince). The mixture should be the consistency of a roughish, loose pesto and take on a strong green colour. Add a generous amount of oil, Parmesan and salt to taste. Again, generosity with the Parmesan takes away the heat of the chilli if you prefer your pesto more mild. I like lots of Parmesan and the heat, too, so sometimes add in more chilli. It is important to taste the pesto to adjust to the balance of flavours to suit you.

Put the pasta into a large saucepan with boiling water, salt and some oil. Cook until al dente, then mix the pasta with the roasted squash and pesto. Serve with some more grated Parmesan. Buon appetito!

Wet polenta with porcini mushrooms

One Italian cook told me that to make real polenta you need to stir it for 2 hours, but I'm afraid I do not have the patience for this. Still, traditional slow-cooking polenta is far creamier than the quick-cooking or instant varieties (considered by some to be a heresy!), and is worth the effort even when you don't make yourself a slave to stirring for hours. This recipe goes very well with meat. Try it with the slow-cooked lamb recipe on page 90 or just some bangers as a fun alternative to bangers and mash. It is also delicious with artichoke hearts.

FEEDS 6–8

500ml milk

200g polenta

110g butter

2 tablespoons olive oil

300g mushrooms, sliced

3 fat garlic cloves, crushed

15g dried porcini mushrooms, soaked in boiling water

80g Parmesan, freshly grated, plus extra for serving

4 tablespoons mascarpone

sea salt

Pour the milk and 700ml water into a large saucepan with a good few pinches of sea salt and bring to the boil. Once boiling, whisk in the polenta. Reduce the heat to low and continue whisking the polenta for 40–50 minutes for slow-cooking polenta, or 20 minutes for quick-cooking, or instant, polenta.

Meanwhile, melt 50g of the butter and the oil in a saucepan. Add the fresh mushroom and sauté for 20 minutes over a medium heat as you are whisking the polenta. When the mushrooms have shrunk and are starting to look rich and brown, stir in the garlic and cook for a minute. Add the porcini mushrooms and their liquid, and simmer for a further 20 minutes over a low heat, allowing you to whisk the polenta at the same time.

When the polenta tastes creamy and is no longer grainy, add the remaining 60g butter, the 80g Parmesan and the mascarpone, and stir through. Stir in the mushroom and taste for seasoning.

Serve on hot plates, drizzled with extra virgin olive oil and with more Parmesan at the table.

Cheat's fazzoletti

Lasagne sheets make the perfect cheat's fazzoletti. Fazzoletti are squares of pasta that you can layer up on a plate with dollops of sauce in between the layers, rather like a relaxed free-form lasagne. Just cook lasagne sheets in salted boiling water until tender, then refresh in cold water. Cut the sheets in half to form squares and layer up with spoonfuls of the mushroom mixture in between each layer of pasta, with freshly grated Parmesan or pecorino sprinkled over the top, and a drizzling of good-quality extra virgin olive oil to finish. This makes a great vegetarian dish.

Hard polenta

When the polenta (with or without the mushrooms) is cooked, pour it into a greased baking dish or gratin dish, and cover with butter papers or greased baking parchment to prevent a skin forming. The polenta will firm up in 30 minutes. It can be grilled or baked in a hot (200°C/400°F/Gas Mark 6) oven until golden, cut into wedges and served with a fresh tomato sauce, basil and buffalo mozzarella, for a lovely summer lunch. Or cut it into smaller pieces and deep-fry (see the recipe for roast pumpkin with deep-fried polenta on page 146).

Roast pumpkin with deep-fried polenta and sage leaves

This is one of my favourite things to eat. The polenta's flavour is perfectly balanced with the sweet pumkin and is delicious with lots of grated Parmesan and a generous drizzling of really good olive oil. A really unusual supper or lunch dish, it also makes a beautiful starter in small quantities.

FEEDS 4

500g pumpkin

1 tablespoon chopped fresh sage plus 20 whole sage leaves

olive oil for cooking

1 quantity of hard polenta (see page 145), cut into 1–2cm cubes

100g freshly grated Parmesan

good-quality extra virgin olive oil for drizzling

sea salt and freshly ground black pepper

Preheat the oven to 200°C/400°F/Gas Mark 6.

Peel the pumpkin and carefully remove all the seeds, taking off all of the stringy pieces of the pumpkin that attach to the seeds. Cut the pumpkin flesh into half-moon slices along the curve, place in a roasting tray and scatter with the chopped sage. Pour in some olive oil and sea salt. Roast in the oven for 30–40 minutes.

Towards the end of the pumpkin's cooking time, heat olive oil to a depth of 3cm in a heavy-bottomed frying pan over a high heat. When the oil is hot (test with a cube of polenta), deep-fry the hard polenta for 5–6 minutes until golden brown, cooking in batches if necessary. Remove with a slotted spoon or tongs, and drain on kitchen paper. Deep-fry the sage leaves, too, taking care not to burn them. Scatter the polenta croutons over the roast pumpkin, together with the Parmesan, a good grind of black pepper, a drizzle of olive oil and the sage leaves. Serve hot or warm.

Green coriander rice

This light and fragrant rice reminds me of my time in Mexico. It is delicious
with stir-fries, simple chicken dishes or as a change from simple steamed rice.

FEEDS 6

1 medium onion, roughly
chopped

2 garlic cloves, chopped

1 large bunch of fresh coriander,
roughly chopped

1 tablespoon olive oil

350g basmati rice, rinsed
and soaked in salted water for
2 hours

1 litre chicken or vegetable stock
(see pages 34 and 35)

Whizz the onion, garlic and coriander in a food processor to
make a green liquid. Heat the oil over a medium heat in a large,
heavy-bottomed saucepan and add the rice, stirring to coat the
grains. Add the onion mixture, and stir around for 2–3 minutes.
Add the stock and cook the rice on low for 25–30 minutes until
the rice is tender, topping up with hot water if needed.

Middle Eastern rice

Melt 80g butter over a medium heat and gently fry ½ cinnamon
stick, the seeds of 5 green cardamom pods and 3 whole black
peppercorns for 3–4 minutes to release their aromas. Stir in
2 tablespoons roughly chopped pine nuts and 2 tablespoons
roughly chopped pistachios, and toast for a few minutes. Rinse
and drain the rice well, add to the same pan and stir for a
minute to coat the grains. Increase the heat to high. Pour
enough water over the rice to cover it roughly by 1cm, and
season with salt. Rest some greaseproof paper on the surface
of the water, then place a lid on the pan, bring to the boil and
simmer for 5 minutes. Remove the lid and paper, and drizzle
the rice with 50ml boiling water infused with a good pinch of
saffron threads. Replace the paper and lid. Reduce the heat and
cook for another 4–5 minutes, then stir in 1 chopped preserved
lemon and 75g raisins. Garnish with fried shallot (see page 28).

Leg of lamb stuffed with Middle Eastern rice

The Middle Eastern rice also makes a spectacular stuffing for
a slow-roasted boned leg of lamb. Add 1 finely chopped red
onion to the cooked Middle Eastern rice. Heat a little olive oil
in a pan and quickly brown the leg all over, then stuff with the
rice. Place the leg of lamb in a roasting tray and roast in the
oven for 4–5 hours at 110°C/225°F/Gas Mark ¼. Delicious!

Quinoa with basil oil and Parmesan

Quinoa is the supergrain from Brazil. It looks a little like couscous, but cooks like rice and is unusual in that it is packed with protein and minerals. It is also delicious when doused in lots of your finest extra virgin olive oil. This recipe is highly versatile. Try it with the spiced lamb on page 88, the fish cakes on page 122 or the pan-fried chicken with walnut sauce on page 103.

FEEDS 6–8

1 litre chicken stock
(see page 34)

500g quinoa

1 quantity of basil oil (see page 37)

75g Parmesan, freshly grated

sea salt and freshly ground
black pepper

Heat the chicken stock in a large saucepan and add the quinoa. Season with salt and pepper. Simmer for 25–30 minutes until the grain still has a little bite, but is tender. You can tell when it is nearly cooked as the grains uncurl and release little tails. You may need to top up with water during the cooking if all the stock has been absorbed.

When the grain is cooked, season with salt and pepper, and toss the quinoa in the basil oil and Parmesan, which will melt into the grains. Serve on warm plates with your accompanying dishes.

Couscous with basil oil and Parmesan

For a much faster version, pour 1 litre hot chicken stock/boiling water over couscous and season with salt and pepper. Leave to stand for 10 minutes, fluffing up with a fork every couple of minutes to prevent clumps forming. Stir in the basil oil and Parmesan, and serve.

Quinoa salad with purple sprouting broccoli and feta

Cook the quinoa as above. Steam 500g purple sprouting broccoli until al dente, about 10 minutes. Chop the broccoli into florets and slice the stalks diagonally. Toss the quinoa in the fattoush dressing on page 186. Stir through the broccoli and 100g crumbled feta.

Lentils with shallots, asparagus and summer herbs

This is a lovely way to eat asparagus when you need to eke it out. The stalks are sliced when they are cooked and tossed through the lentils, which makes a lovely soupy vegetable dish. All you need is some grilled chicken and a wedge of lemon for a perfect simple summer supper.

FEEDS 4–6

2 tablespoons olive oil

4 shallots or 1 medium onion, finely chopped

1 small carrot, finely chopped

2 celery sticks, chopped

2 garlic cloves, finely chopped

2 bay leaves

50g streaky bacon, finely chopped (optional)

350g Puy lentils

zest and juice of 1 lemon

500ml chicken or vegetable stock (see pages 34 and 35)

150g frozen peas

12 asparagus stalks

1 tablespoon chopped fresh chervil

1 tablespoon chopped fresh thyme

1 tablespoon chopped fresh marjoram

1 tablespoon basil oil (optional, see page 39)

sea salt and freshly ground black pepper

extra virgin olive oil to serve

Heat the olive oil in a heavy frying pan over a medium heat and add the shallot, carrot, celery, garlic, bay leaves and bacon (if using). Sauté for 5 minutes before adding the lentils and lemon zest, stirring well. Add the stock and peas, and bring to a simmer. Simmer until the lentils are just tender but not collapsed and the stock has been absorbed (20–30 minutes).

In a separate pan (use a tall, slender asparagus pan if you have one), steam the asparagus over simmering water until the stalks are almost tender, 5–8 minutes. It is important here not to overcook the asparagus because it is going to be tossed in with the lentils and heated through again, which will continue its cooking. Remove the asparagus from the pan when it still has a bite to it and refresh in cold water to stop the cooking process. Slice into 1cm diagonal chunks.

Add the asparagus pieces to the lentils together with the chopped herbs. Squeeze over half the lemon juice and check the seasoning. Drizzle with the basil oil, if using, and a little of your finest extra virgin olive oil and serve. This is exceptionally good with grilled chicken or pan-fried fish. You can also add a splash of walnut oil to give it a more robust flavour.

Lentils with roast garlic, Jerusalem artichokes and goat's cheese

Omit the asparagus and peel and slice 250g Jerusalem artichokes instead. Add to the sautéing vegetables for 5 minutes before adding the lentils, then continue cooking as above. Serve with 200g creamy goat's cheese and 3–4 seasoned heads of garlic, sliced across the middle, drizzled with olive oil and roasted in a preheated hot (200°C/400°F/Gas Mark 6) oven for 15–20 minutes until soft.

Saffron cannellini beans with fruit alioli

While I often use tins of beans in recipes for speed, here I like to go the whole hog and soak dried cannellini beans overnight. Buy them as new as you can. Their flavour will be richer and creamier than ones that have been sitting around for a long time and much better than the tinned ones. This recipe was inspired by Stephanie Alexander's *The Cook's Companion*. It melts in the mouth and is a brilliant accompaniment to roast chicken.

FEEDS 6

400g dried cannellini beans, soaked in cold water overnight

pinch of bicarbonate of soda

2 carrots

3 medium onions

3 celery sticks

3 garlic cloves, all halved, for the cooking water

3 bay leaves

1 tablespoon extra virgin olive oil

small pinch of saffron threads

sprig of fresh parsley

a few sprigs of fresh thyme

200ml chicken stock

about 2 tablespoons freshly grated Parmesan

1 quantity of fruit alioli (see page 76)

sea salt and freshly ground black pepper

Rinse the beans and put them in a large pan. Cover with water and add the bicarbonate of soda. Take 1 peeled carrot, 1 peeled onion, 2 celery sticks and 2 peeled garlic cloves, halved, and add to the cooking water with 2 of the bay leaves. Simmer for 1½–2 hours, uncovered, skimming off any scum that rises to the surface, until the beans are just cooked and tender. Drain, discarding the vegetables.

Dice the remaining 2 onions and sweat them in the olive oil over a medium heat until turning translucent. Dice the remaining carrot and celery stick, and crush the remaining garlic clove. Add to the onion with the saffron, remaining bay leaf, parsley and thyme, and sweat for 15 minutes until the vegetables are tender. Add the cooked beans and chicken stock. Cook gently until most of the stock has been absorbed.

Stir in a good grating of Parmesan (about 2 tablespoons) and 50ml of the fruit alioli. Season with salt and pepper. Serve in warm bowls with more fruit alioli drizzled over the top.

If you are serving the beans with roast chicken (do try it), arrange the beans on a large platter with the chicken carved, jointed and laid out on top, and the extra alioli drizzled over the chicken and the beans.

Cannellini beans with sautéed vegetables

Add slices of parboiled, sliced Jerusalem artichokes, globe artichoke hearts, asparagus or pumpkin to the sweating onions and garlic, depending on the season. If you are using spring vegetables, you can make the fruit alioli with 1 tablespoon apricot purée instead of apple, pear or quince.

Vegetables

It is funny how growing up with the old British stereotype of meat and two veg affects your way of thinking. I used to think about vegetables in that light – as an add-on to the main ingredient on the plate, be it fish or meat. It is amazing how you can still eat vegetables in this same style, up and down the British Isles. Lots of care and attention is given to the main ingredient, with the vegetables tacked on as an afterthought, sometimes on a separate plate, and either boiled like mad and therefore soggy, with all the vitamins and minerals drained away, or almost raw, unseasoned and tasteless.

But, no! Vegetables are our seasons. We have such a variety of fresh, local vegetables (not to mention fruit) in the United Kingdom that we can constantly enjoy new ways to eat them, without always having to resort to those that are air-freighted, year-round, from far-flung parts of the globe. The seasons are what make our island so special. Each one brings the birth of a fresh cycle of new crops. It is such fun when the first globe artichokes appear in the markets and I dream about dunking the hearts in delicious beurre noir. Or there is the time when the first spring vegetables appear – you can sit in the early sunshine munching beautifully cooked asparagus, new potatoes, baby carrots and raw baby broad beans, all dipped into a fresh aïoli or lemon mayonnaise. These are utterly delicious when properly cooked, don't cost too much and take no time to prepare. In the winter we can comfort ourselves with all our amazing root vegetables as we hibernate from the cold. Sweet parsnips, nutty celeriac and delicious squashes. Each vegetable can be multiplied endlessly by the number of ways you can eat it.

I grew into vegetables thanks to Jane Grigson's *Vegetable Book*, Alice L Waters's *Chez Panisse Vegetables*, Dennis Cotter's amazing vegetarian cooking in Ireland and the *River Cafe Cookbook Green* – I am now a complete convert. It is a great tribute to the Italian influence on our cooking that we now so often have courses entirely devoted to vegetables. I can think of no better starter than a plate of just-cooked broccoli, sprinkled with shaved pecorino and chopped anchovies, and a slosh of new season's olive oil. Unless perhaps it is roast aubergine with feta and chilli. Or maybe curly kale, chopped and tossed in penne, with a good grating of fresh Parmesan. Many of the dishes in this chapter can be side dishes or starters depending on your mood.

To get the absolute most out of the vegetables you buy and the best value for money, I would urge you to visit a greengrocer, a farm shop or a farmers' market whenever you can. It is here that you can see vegetables at their best, and everything looking like it should – freshly picked from the ground.

Char-grilled courgette wedges with basil, mint, chilli and lemon

This is a light, zingy way to serve courgettes. It is simple to cook and yet never fails to get people excited. It can also be made in advance and eaten at room temperature as a summer salad.

FEEDS 4–6

6 courgettes, ends trimmed and cut into long diagonal slices, about 2cm wide

1–2 tablespoons extra virgin olive oil plus extra for dressing

1 fresh red chilli, seeded and finely chopped, or ½ teaspoon dried chilli flakes

juice of ½ lemon

good handful of roughly chopped fresh mint

good handful of roughly chopped fresh basil

sea salt and freshly ground black pepper

You will need a ridged grill pan or char-grill for cooking the courgette. Toss the courgette strips in a bowl with the 1–2 tablespoons olive oil (just enough to coat the courgette), chilli, salt and pepper.

Heat the grill pan until smoking hot and cook the courgettes in batches, about 4 minutes a side. They should be tender, but with a crunch to them in the middle. If the strips are not quite cooked, leave them on the char-grill for longer, but watch the heat as you don't want them to burn. Don't be tempted to move the courgette while it is cooking or you won't get the char-grill marks across the flesh. Drain on kitchen paper.

Adjust seasoning if necessary, and toss in the lemon juice, mint, basil and a good slug of your best extra virgin olive oil.

Variations

These char-grilled courgette strips are delicious mixed with feta, rocket and other green leaves as a warm salad. Or substitute them, along with feta or goat's cheese, in the basic frittata recipe on page 56 for a fast, delicious supper. Alternatively, cook some penne pasta until al dente. Quickly toss the pasta with a garlic paste made from 1 mashed garlic clove and some Maldon sea salt, and the courgette strips. Add 100g toasted pine nuts and serve at once for a quick and easy pasta dish.

Fennel gratin

I love eating fennel when it is crunchy and crispy, as it is in the salad on page 178, but it is also delicious soft, melted and caramelised.

FEEDS 4-6

4 lage fennel bulbs

50g butter

50ml white wine

240ml water or chicken or vegetable stock (see pages 34-35)

small handful of fresh thyme, leaves picked and chopped

generous handful of chopped fresh flat-leaf parsley

240ml double cream

handful of stale breadcrumbs (see note below)

50-100g Parmesan, freshly grated

sea salt and freshly ground black pepper

Preheat the oven to 190°C/375°F/Gas Mark 5.

Trim the ends off the fennel, reserving the top stalks and fronds for salads. Cut the bulbs into quarters lengthways.

Melt the butter in an ovenproof casserole dish large enough to hold the fennel. Add the fennel, season and sauté over a medium-high heat for 10 minutes until the fennel starts to brown and caramelise. Add the wine, stock, thyme and parsley, and bring to a simmer. Drizzle with the cream, then scatter over the breadcrumbs and a generous amount of Parmesan. Transfer the dish to the oven. Bake for 40 minutes until golden and bubbling. Serve either hot or at room temperature.

Braised fennel

For braised fennel, follow the method as far as adding the wine and stock, then simmer uncovered until the liquid has reduced to a thick syrup, before adding a splash of Pernod to bring out the anise flavour in the fennel. Serve with steak or roast pork.

Bread, croutons and breadcrumbs

A good loaf of bread can metamorphose into croutons and breadcrumbs with the slice of a knife or the pulse of a food processor. Without good country-style or sourdough bread there would be no toasted ciabatta croutons, saturated in olive oil, garlic and Parmesan, to fill out a skinny salad. No instantaneous lunch of toast rubbed with garlic, drenched in olive oil and topped with delectable ingredients (pages 22-7). No crostini rustled up in a jiffy for friends (pages 18-19). Make a point of whizzing up leftover bits of stale bread in the food processor. Leave the breadcrumbs to dry in a cool oven and store in old jam jars. Perfect for fish cakes, gratins, herby crusts on pasta (page 136), garlicky toppings on fried eggs, indulgent treacle tarts or fried wedges of pecorino.

Spinach with shallots and nutmeg

Baby spinach is delicious raw in salads with crispy bacon and toasted walnuts, but I love cooked spinach, too. This recipe takes 5 minutes and is mouth-watering. Put it on toast with a poached egg on top for eggs Florentine, or just serve it as a vegetable. Either way it is full of iron and goodness.

FEEDS 6

1 tablespoon olive oil

2 shallots, chopped

1 garlic clove, finely chopped

600g fresh spinach, thoroughly rinsed and dried

grind of nutmeg

splash of sherry vinegar or a squeeze of lemon juice

sea salt and freshly ground black pepper

Heat the olive oil in your biggest pan over a medium-high heat and add the shallot. Cook for 5 minutes until the shallot is turning translucent, then add the garlic. Sweat for a minute before adding all the spinach. Stir over the heat until the spinach has collapsed, about 5 minutes. Grate some nutmeg over the spinach, and season with salt and pepper. Add a splash of sherry vinegar for flavour and serve.

Sicilian broccoli

Broccoli is one of my favourite vegetables, particularly the stem, which I think has so much of the flavour. Apparently it is also one of those cancer-beating superfoods. All the more reason for loving it.

FEEDS 4

450g broccoli

3 tablespoons extra virgin olive oil

½ large fresh red chilli, seeded and finely chopped

2 garlic cloves, sliced

4 anchovy fillets, drained of oil and finely chopped

50g black olives, pitted and chopped

60g Parmesan, finely grated

squeeze of lemon juice

sea salt and freshly ground black pepper

Peel the tough, outer skin of the broccoli stalk. Slice into rounds about ½cm thick up to the head. Cut the florets into small clusters. Steam the broccoli until al dente, 7–10 minutes. Transfer to a warm, shallow dish.

In a separate pan, warm the oil and add the chilli and garlic. Sweat for 1–2 minutes (do not burn!). Scatter the broccoli with the anchovies and olives, and drizzle over the garlic oil. Sprinkle with the Parmesan and place under a hot grill for a couple of minutes to melt the cheese. Season with the lemon juice, salt and pepper. Serve immediately.

Sicilian broccoli with penne

Cook the broccoli as above and toss with penne pasta cooked until al dente. Drizzle with extra virgin olive oil and serve with freshly grated nutmeg and more freshly grated Parmesan.

Broccoli pesto with penne

Steam the broccoli as per the instructions above. Cut the clusters in half and toss in penne pasta cooked until al dente and some home-made pesto (see page 70).

My baba ganoush

I make this simple and seriously good recipe when I have only 20 minutes to spare and need something healthy to eat, or just want to add a delicious dip to a spread of dishes. I made this the other day mixed up with equal parts of humus, together with a tomato and red onion salad and some pitta bread. It is also the most incredible stuffing for a leg of lamb (see page 86). In the Balkans they mix a dip similar to this with walnut paste. I experimented with the walnut paste on page 103 and found it utterly delicious. Baba ganoush is lovely with tzatziki, lamb, flatbread and masses of feta salad for a picnic.

FEEDS 4–6

1 large aubergine

2 tablespoons tahini

juice of ½ lemon

1 garlic clove, crushed with Maldon sea salt

1 tablespoon best-quality extra virgin olive oil you can find (see note)

1 teaspoon freshly ground cumin seed (optional)

sea salt and freshly ground black pepper

Hold the aubergine by the stalk and place over a gas flame, turning regularly until the skin blackens and blisters all over, about 8 minutes. Alternatively, wrap in foil and bake in a preheated hot (200°C/400°F/Gas Mark 6) oven for 20 minutes. Peel with care (it gets pretty hot!) and put the flesh in a bowl with the tahini, lemon juice, garlic, olive oil and ground cumin, if using. Season to taste. This keeps well in the refrigerator, but is best eaten at room temperature.

Olive oil

I think it's worth investing in the best olive oil you can afford. Whenever I go home I argue with my mother about olive oil. She always asks me how she's supposed to know a good extra virgin olive oil when she sees one. I always tell her just to buy a bottle and taste it. If you like it you can buy it again; if you don't, you can have an adventure with a new kind.

I love a good extra virgin olive oil so much that I can dribble it on a tomato with a pinch of salt and have it for breakfast. Douse it over some melted dark chocolate on toast (see page 212), or just mop it up with masses of bread. When browning meat or deep-frying fish or chips I use normal olive oil. When sweating vegetables or pan-frying meat or fish I would use a bog-standard extra virgin for some added flavour. I never cook with a top-notch, expensive extra virgin olive oil. Rather, this comes into its own fresh and unadulterated, when drizzled, doused or dipped.

Roast aubergine with pomegranate, feta and mint

This is a truly delicious dish to give to your friends. Middle Eastern-inspired, it goes beautifully with a whole table of mezze. I made it once for a boyfriend's birthday. We had masses of people crammed into his flat and I remember being terrified I wouldn't have enough to feed everyone. Try cooking it with Middle Eastern rice (see page 148), slow-cooked lamb (pages 85–6) and fattoush (page 186). We made fairly good inroads into it all before the dancing started, but the plate that was really demolished was this one. It is also a great vegetarian dish served simply with rice. I love it with flavourful ripe tomatoes instead of pomegranate at the height of summer.

FEEDS 4–6

1 garlic clove

juice of ½ lemon

best-quality extra virgin olive oil (see page 159)

250g feta, cubed

large handful of fresh mint, chopped

1 large fresh red chilli, seeded and finely chopped

4 smallish aubergines, halved lengthways

2 teaspoons cumin seed, warmed and crushed

seeds from 1 pomegranate

Maldon sea salt and freshly ground black pepper

To make the marinated feta, use a mortar and pestle to crush the garlic to a paste with a good few pinches of Maldon sea salt. Add the lemon juice and a good glug of your finest extra virgin olive oil (1–2 tablespoons). Toss the feta lightly in the dressing together with the mint and chilli. Season with black pepper and cover with more extra virgin olive oil, leaving the feta to marinate in your refrigerator for a few hours or preferably overnight.

To prepare the aubergine, preheat the oven to 200°C/400°F/Gas Mark 6. Make diagonal crisscross slashes on the cut side of the aubergines and season with salt and pepper. Heat 2 tablespoons olive oil in the frying pan and fry the aubergine in batches that fit the pan, cut-side down, for 5–10 minutes, until beautifully golden, adding more olive oil if necessary. Turn the aubergine, cut-side up, into a shallow baking tray and sprinkle with the cumin. Pop in the oven for 25 minutes until the flesh is soft.

When you are ready to eat, arrange the aubergine on a large serving plate or platter. Toss the marinated feta with the pomegranate seeds and taste for seasoning. It may need to be balanced with the other flavours; experiment to see what you like best. Sprinkle the feta salad over the aubergine and let its colours decorate the table.

Variation

In the summer, substitute the pomegranate for 3 very ripe tomatoes, skinned (see page 136), seeded and finely chopped. I tend to sprinkle over a small pinch of soft brown sugar, to bring out the sweetness of the tomato.

Tommi's tip

Always ask a greengrocer to cut open a pomegranate for you first so that you can be sure to get the brilliant red seeds. The flavour of pomegranates is rich and fruity at the height of their season through the winter months. To remove pomegranate seeds with minimum effort, roll the fruit around on a work surface with your hand pressed firmly down on it. This pressure will release the seeds from the bitter white pith. Cut across the circumference and the seeds and juice should fall out of the fruit.

Curly kale with olive oil and garlic

Curly kale is from the Brassica family of vegetables, is extremely good for you and, like broccoli, is reputed to be a real cancer-beater. I love eating food that I know is doing me good as long as it is delicious as well. I think this is quite the best way to cook kale. It is inspired by my flatmate Joe's Italian cooking. He does this at the River Café with cavolo nero, which is a delicious Italian winter leaf, but it works just as well with curly kale and transforms this rather under-appreciated vegetable into a dish you will want to devour. It also takes minutes to cook.

FEEDS 4–6

3 tablespoons olive oil

1 large head of curly kale, stem discarded, leaves rinsed and roughly chopped

3 garlic cloves, thinly sliced on the diagonal

1 fresh red chilli, seeded and chopped (optional)

juice of ½ lemon

sea salt and freshly ground black pepper

Heat the olive oil in a large saucepan or wok until really hot, and add the kale (it makes a great sizzling noise). Give it a good stir and add the garlic and chilli, if you like a bit of kick. Stir-fry for 7–8 minutes, taking care not to burn the garlic, then season with salt and pepper, and sprinkle over the lemon juice. Then eat up your greens!

Curly kale soup with olive oil and garlic
Toss 3 or 4 sliced potatoes (scrubbed but not peeled) in olive oil over a medium heat, and sauté without colouring for 5 minutes before turning up the heat and adding the kale. Cook as above, adding 1.5 litres good-quality chicken or vegetable stock (see pages 34 and 35) after 5 minutes. Simmer until the potato is tender, about 15 minutes. Serve in soup bowls drizzled with plenty of fruity extra virgin olive oil and good crusty bread.

Penne with curly kale and sautéed celeriac
Cook the kale as above. Sauté 1cm cubes of celeriac in a little olive oil until tender. Toss the kale and 2–3 tablespoons toasted pine nuts into the celeriac. Meanwhile, cook some penne pasta until al dente. Serve the kale and celeriac tossed through the hot pasta with dollops of very ripe Gorgonzola. Or serve as a starter without the pasta.

All things mashed

There is nothing quite so comforting as a plate of piping-hot mashed potato. I have recently branched out, though, and have discovered that celeriac mash (great with venison) and sweet potato mash have their place upon the pedestal, too. Celeriac brings its celery flavour with a hint of nuttiness to the dish, while the sweet potato here is spicy and sweet. I also love a smooth cauliflower mash. It is delicious with the braised rabbit on page 97 and also the lamb klefticon on page 90. Try the variations below with different meat dishes to ring the changes.

ALL SERVE 6–8

1kg floury potatoes, peeled and cut into even chunks
50g butter
100ml warmed milk
1–2 tablespoons double cream
good grinding of fresh nutmeg
salt and pepper

Classic potato mash

Steam the potatoes until tender, about 20 minutes. Mash thoroughly, then pass through a sieve or potato ricer if you have one – this will get rid of all the lumps.

Once the potatoes are smooth, beat in the butter and hot milk. Add the cream and season to taste with plenty of nutmeg, salt and pepper. Serve at once to ensure a light, fluffy mash.

Variations
Potatoes duchesse – beat in an egg yolk with the butter and milk.
Roast garlic mash – roast 1 head of garlic, drizzled in olive oil, in a hot oven (200°C/400°F/Gas Mark 6) for 20 minutes. Peel, mash with a fork and mix into the potatoes.
Wild garlic mash – mix in 1–2 tablespoons finely chopped wild garlic.
Spring onion and cheddar mash – mix in 1–2 tablespoons finely chopped spring onion and 100g grated extra-mature cheddar.

Tommi's tip
Steaming the potato instead of boiling it means that the potato does not become waterlogged. The result is a lovely fluffy mash, without it being sloppy.

Celeriac, potato and Dijon mustard mash

600g floury potatoes, peeled and cut into even chunks

1 medium celeriac, peeled and cut into even chunks

220ml crème fraîche

1 heaped teaspoon Dijon mustard

1 teaspoon horseradish cream (see page 16) (optional)

sea salt and freshly ground black pepper

Steam the potato and celeriac for 20 minutes or until tender.

Heat the crème fraîche, Dijon mustard and horseradish cream, if using, in a small pan until almost simmering.

Mash the vegetables as normal and season with salt and pepper. Add the warm cream mixture once the mash is smooth. Adjust seasoning if necessary. This mash is delicious with the rich oxtail stew on page 91.

Sweet potato, maple syrup and chilli mash

500g sweet potatoes, peeled and cut into chunks

300g floury potatoes, peeled, cut into chunks and steamed as above

2 fresh red chillies, seeded and chopped

1 tablespoon maple syrup

1 teaspoon light soy sauce

1 teaspoon saba (see note) or balsamic vinegar

3 tablespoons olive oil

3 garlic cloves, peeled

100ml warmed milk

50g butter

2 tablespoons crème fraîche

sea salt and freshly ground black pepper

Preheat the oven to 210°C/410°F/Gas Mark 6–7.

Put the sweet potato and potato in a roasting tin and sprinkle with the chilli, maple syrup, soy sauce and saba. Drizzle over the olive oil. Roast in the oven until slightly blackened and tender, about 30 minutes, adding the garlic cloves halfway through the cooking time.

Take out and mash or whizz in a food processor with the milk, butter and crème fraîche. Season with salt and pepper.

Note Saba is a syrup made from cooked grapes. It is treacly in flavour (a little like a properly aged balsamic vinegar) and adds depth to sauces, glazes and gravies. It can be found in the vinegar section of most good supermarkets.

Smooth cauliflower mash

100g butter

350g cauliflower, broken into florets

1 large onion, finely chopped

2 medium floury potatoes, peeled and diced

2 parsnips, diced

100ml warmed milk

sea salt and freshly ground black pepper

Melt most of the butter in a pan over a medium heat. Add the cauliflower, onion, potato and parsnip. Season to taste and sauté until the vegetables are quite soft and starting to caramelise – this will add a deliciously nutty flavour to your mash. Whizz using a hand-held electric wand or in a food processor. For a really smooth purée, rub the mixture through a sieve. This mash is delicious served with stews.

Crispy, garlicky potatoes

These potatoes are the easiest things in the world to make and irresistible, as you might expect from the marriage of garlic, olive oil, potatoes and sage. Once they have gone into the oven you can forget about them until they are done and fill your kitchen with their intoxicating smell.

FEEDS 4–6

1.5kg potatoes (you can use floury or waxy here), peeled and cut into 2cm chunks

80ml olive oil (I like to use a standard-quality extra virgin here – see page 159)

8–10 garlic cloves, peeled but left whole

grated zest of 1 lemon

8–10 fresh sage leaves, roughly chopped

Preheat the oven to 220°–230°C/425°–450°F/Gas Mark 7–8. Put the potatoes into a large pan of cold, salted water and bring to the boil. Simmer for 5 minutes, then drain.

Pour the olive oil into a roasting tin and heat over a moderate heat with the garlic for about 5 minutes, until the garlic has taken on some colour (and flavoured the oil). Remove the cloves with a slotted spoon and set aside. Toss the potato chunks in the hot oil and add the lemon zest. Roast the chunks in the oven for about 25 minutes before adding the garlic cloves and sage leaves, stirring to mix through. Roast for about another 20 minutes until the potato chunks are crisp, golden and smelling deliciously of sage and garlic. Eat at once, as a snack, or as a side vegetable, or top with Taleggio, mature cheddar, brie or another favourite cheese, and pop back in the oven for another 5 minutes. Serve as a simple supper dish with a light green salad.

Note Light, floury potato varieties such as King Edward, or the versatile Desiree and Maris Piper (the latter two also make good chips), are great for mashing or roasting. Waxy potatoes such as Charlottes or Marfonas are good varieties to use when making chips, boiling or using potatoes in salads.

Layered potatoes with sage and fruit alioli

This is such a good way to do potatoes. It is similar to dauphinoise, although for some reason cooking it in alioli instead of the more traditional cream reduces the cooking time considerably. You can add quite a garlicky alioli to this, as the flavour mellows during the cooking.

FEEDS 4

900g potatoes such as King Edward or Maris Piper, peeled and very thinly sliced (about ½cm thick)

a little olive oil

just over ½ quantity of fruit alioli (see page 76)

large bunch of fresh sage, chopped

sea salt and freshly ground black pepper

Preheat the oven to 200°C/400°F/Gas Mark 6.

Lightly grease a baking dish (about 22 x 33 x 5cm) with a little olive oil. Layer the potato in the dish, overlapping the edges slightly and interspersing each layer with small dollops of the alioli and scatterings of sage, and seasoning with salt and pepper as you go. Bake in the oven for 35 minutes. The potatoes will be crispy on top and soft and gooey underneath. Serve hot.

Parmesan, parsnip and fruit alioli layer cake

Peel 6 large parsnips and cut lengthways into slices about ½cm thick, then thinly slice 1 onion. Layer the parsnip in a baking dish as above, interspersing each layer with the onion, some fruit alioli and salt and pepper to taste. Top with 100g freshly grated Parmesan and bake for 35 minutes. My nephew pronounced this utterly yummy and it goes well with roast meats, particularly the slow-cooked lamb on page 85–6.

Salads and salad dressings

Salads are a favourite of mine. They can be light or filling, can be served as a starter or to follow a rich main course, or can be eaten with a piece of fish. I can feast quite happily on a huge plate of green salad with a chunk of delicious mature cheddar and some fresh bread. Add some pickle and I'm in heaven.

Salads can be made out of pretty much anything. When I am working from home I have often come up with extraordinary mixes of ingredients I have found lurking in my fridge which, when steamed a little, or chopped or shaved or fried, suddenly become lunch. A few scattered toasted pumpkin seeds or walnuts add substance and a little extra protein. Rich in omega-3 oils, they also reputedly keep your brain sharp and your mood buoyant (anything that can keep me buoyant over long British winters has to be appreciated).

Salads are also great for naturally greedy people. I find I can eat plates and plates of salad and still feel charged. I don't mean rabbit food either. When I think of my favourite salads they are studded with dollops of blue cheese or goat's cheese. Warm potato salads or salads with roasted parsnips are among my favourites, but add some lentils to some rocket and I'm still happy. Partridge or pigeon breasts fried for a few minutes are a perfect accompaniment to piles of watercress, spinach, rocket or baby gem. With salads your creativity is boundless.

If you like fast food with no fuss, there are a few ingredients that I would always have in my cupboard for salad moments. A really good bottle of extra virgin olive oil will transform even the humblest ingredients. I am also mad about walnut oil, although there is a huge difference between the good and the bad. This is one of the things I splash a bit of extra money on – try a rich, toasty-flavoured walnut oil on the Jerusalem artichoke salad on page 178 and you really will feel your spirits lift. There is a huge difference in vinegars, too, just as a cheap wine will not taste as good as a better quality one (the word vinegar does come from the French, which translates as bitter wine). My staple vinegars are sherry vinegar and a good Cabernet red wine vinegar, but I can't do without good balsamic and white wine vinegars either, while rice wine vinegar is great to sprinkle onto Asian dishes. Raisins, nuts and seeds are also very useful to keep for salads, as are anchovies and capers. I also always have a large wedge of Parmigiano-Reggiano sitting in my fridge. Wrapped in waxed or greaseproof paper, it lasts for ages and is always on hand to jazz up salad leaves or a vinaigrette.

Onions, whether red, spring or shallot, are also important, but nearly lost me a boyfriend a few years back. Now I macerate them in salad dressing for 10 minutes before eating and find that their antisocial aftertaste is completely eradicated. Perfect.

Six good salad dressings

Below are some of my favourite salad dressings. Dressing salad leaves can be as simple as sprinkling with a good quality extra virgin olive oil and some lemon juice, or you can go to town with a walnut oil vinaigrette. The choice is yours, but always try to use the best-quality oils and vinegars – it will reflect in the taste of the dressing. Never forget to season a salad with salt and pepper – the best dressing in the world falls flat without seasoning.

Classic French dressing with shallots

MAKES ABOUT 100ML DRESSING

3 shallots, sliced wafer thin
1 teaspoon grainy mustard
1 tablespoon brown sugar
25ml white wine vinegar
large pinch of Maldon sea salt
5 good grinds of black pepper
75ml extra virgin olive oil

Mix all the ingredients except the olive oil in a glass jar with a screwtop lid. Shake well, to dissolve the sugar. Let sit for 10 minutes (this takes the onion punch out of the shallot and softens its flavour). Add the oil and shake again just before dressing your salad. I sometimes add a splash of balsamic vinegar for added sweetness, or use red wine or sherry vinegar instead of the white wine to suit my mood. Red wine vinegar has a more rounded flavour than white wine vinegar, with a bit more body, while sherry vinegar has a lovely sweet tang. This keeps for 2–3 days in the refrigerator.

Walnut oil dressing

MAKES ABOUT 100ML DRESSING

1 teaspoon Dijon mustard
large pinch of Maldon sea salt
5 grinds of black pepper
½ teaspoon runny honey
25ml white wine vinegar
75ml walnut oil (the best you can find)

Mix all the ingredients except the walnut oil in a glass jar with a screwtop lid. Shake well, to dissolve the honey and salt. Stir in the oil, shake and use to dress your salad.

Skye's simple lemon juice and extra virgin olive oil dressing

MAKES 1 SERVING

1 lemon
best-quality extra virgin olive oil
freshly grated or shaved Parmesan
Maldon sea salt and freshly ground black pepper

Zest a lemon, cut it in half and squeeze the juice over your salad. Douse with the finest extra virgin olive oil you can lay your hands on, then sprinkle with some grated Parmesan, the lemon zest and plenty of salt and pepper.

Bagna cauda dressing

MAKES ABOUT 100ML

8–10 large anchovy fillets, drained of oil

1 or 2 large garlic cloves, any green inner stem removed

good pinch of sugar

good squeeze of lemon juice

75ml extra virgin olive oil

freshly ground black pepper

Mash the anchovies and garlic using a mortar and pestle, to make a smooth paste. Add the sugar and lemon juice, and gently mash in the oil to form an emulsion. Season with pepper. This dressing is delicious on steamed broccoli. Try adding 50g ground toasted walnuts for more body.

Chipotle dressing

MAKES ABOUT 150ML

50ml balsamic vinegar

1–2 tablespoons chipotle en adobo, depending on love of heat (see page 75)

juice of 1 lemon

2 teaspoons rice vinegar

1 teaspoon sesame oil

1½ teaspoons honey

75ml olive oil

Put the dressing ingredients in a glass jar with a screwtop lid and shake to mix well. If you can't get hold of the chipotle en adobo, you can substitute it with 1 fresh red chilli, seeded and minced with 1 tablespoon pimentón dulce (sweet smoked paprika) (see page 121).

Vietnamese salad dressing

MAKES ABOUT 100ML

2 tablespoons palm sugar or soft brown sugar

1 tablespoon fish sauce

1 tablespoon light soy sauce

2 tablespoons freshly squeezed lime juice

1 small fresh red chilli, seeded and finely chopped

1 garlic clove, crushed

1 teaspoon rice vinegar

a few drops of sesame oil

Dissolve the palm sugar in the fish sauce, soy sauce and lime juice, then combine with the rest of the ingredients. Adjust the seasoning if necessary – you want a balance of sweet, salty and sour. This salad dressing goes with lots of different dishes. I particularly like it on a salad of shaved raw carrot, celeriac and parsnip, with some fried shrimp. A really good warming winter salad dish.

Beetroot, rocket and goat's cheese salad

This is a delicious salad that perfectly balances the sweet flavour of the beetroot with the earthy goat's cheese and the tang of the vinegar dressing. It is so good that I love it on bruschetta, too (see page 27 for a similar version).

FEEDS 4

500g beetroot

1 quantity of walnut oil dressing or French dressing with shallots (see page 174)

250g rocket

2 spring onions, finely chopped

80g pumpkin seeds, toasted

100g goat's cheese

1 teaspoon reduced balsamic vinegar (see page 80)

sea salt and freshly ground black pepper

Cut off the leaves of the beetroot, leaving at least 2 cm of the stalk. Do not cut off the tails. Simmer the beetroot in salted boiling water until a knife can pierce them without resistance – the timing will depend on the size of the beetroot. If they are baby ones, they may take only 30 minutes; if they are large, they can take up to 1½ hours. When they are cooked, slip off the skins, wearing rubber gloves to avoid staining your hands. Cut into small 2cm wedges and, while still warm, toss with half the walnut dressing or the classic French dressing, but using red wine vinegar in place of white wine vinegar if using the latter.

Next toss the beetroot, rocket, spring onion and pumpkin seeds in a salad bowl with the rest of the dressing. Season with salt and pepper. Crumble the goat's cheese over the top and drizzle with the reduced balsamic vinegar.

Caramelised parsnip, beetroot and rocket salad

Parboil equal quantities of parsnip and beetroot, and sauté in 50g butter over a medium-high heat for 10 minutes, so that the vegetables caramelise in the hot butter. Toss the vegetables in half the quantity of the dressing, then with the remaining ingredients (including the rest of the dressing), as above.

Jerusalem artichoke, fennel and Parmesan salad with walnut oil dressing

I love Jerusalem artichokes and a bonus is that they have two seasons: one in the winter and a brief reappearance in the spring. Sweating them in oil and slicing them into lentils or rice, or puréeing them in soup both bring out their flavour. They are also delectable char-grilled, with the smokiness enhancing their taste. In the spring you can slice them raw, as their flavour remains light and delicate, and goes beautifully with other subtle vegetables. This version is inspired by an incredible salad we served at Petersham with fresh porcini mushrooms and slivers of sweet Parma ham, and it makes a lovely spring starter. I use wafer-thin slices of fennel bulb instead; fennel is another one of my favourite vegetables and a perfect accompaniment to the subtle artichoke flavour. Try matching this with the cheese soufflé on pages 58–9 for a truly magical feast. If you have problems with the aftereffects of Jerusalem artichokes, follow the asafoetida tip on page 38.

FEEDS 6

450g Jerusalem artichokes
450g fennel
juice of 1 lemon
80g Parmesan
small bunch of fresh curly parsley, finely chopped
1 quantity of walnut oil dressing (see page 174)

Thinly slice or shave the artichokes and fennel, sprinkling with the lemon juice as you cut them to stop them discolouring. They can be kept prepared like this in the refrigerator for a few hours before eating. Just before serving, shave the Parmesan into fine slivers and toss into the salad, together with the parsley and walnut dressing.

Walnuts

Walnuts happily are not only delicious but also entirely good for you. They are full of omega-3 but unlike fish not in danger of extinction (yet), so you can eat them like crazy all through winter to ward off the blues. They are delicious in many different salads (see pages 179 and 183). Or try them toasted in your porridge for breakfast. I'll eat handfuls from the cupboard with a few dates or dried apricots for an impromptu healthy snack. Walnuts are exceptionally wicked coated in caramel or melted chocolate, and they are great with fried fish or chicken (pages 103–5). Delicious, sexy, brain food – what more could you ask for in a nut?

Char-grilled winter vegetables with blue cheese

I first read about char-grilling Jerusalem artichokes in Fergus Henderson's wonderful *Nose to Tail Eating* while I was competing on *MasterChef Goes Large*. I was trying to find a starter to get me through to the semifinals when I stumbled upon this way of cooking them – it seemed like a moment of divine intervention (which is quite normal with Fergus's food). Char-grilling vegetables brings out their natural sugars and it does truly magical things to Jerusalem artichokes. It is also a delicious way of cooking chicory. I gave this to Hugh and the rest of the *Soup Kitchen* team for a starter one night to say thank you, and even my flatmate, Joe, looked proud of me.

FEEDS 6

5 Jerusalem artichokes, scrubbed but not peeled

3 heads of chicory, tailed and quartered lengthways

3 tablespoons olive oil

200g rocket

150g Cashel blue cheese

80g walnuts, toasted

2 tablespoons chopped fresh flat-leaf parsley (optional)

For the dressing

50ml walnut oil

1 teaspoon red wine vinegar

juice of 1 lemon

1 teaspoon Dijon mustard

pinch of sugar

sea salt and freshly ground black pepper

You will need a ridged pan or griddle for char-grilling the vegetables.

Simmer the artichokes for 10 minutes in salted water until just tender (be careful not to overcook them or they will collapse), and cut into 1cm wide slices. Toss the artichokes and chicory in the olive oil, season and cook on a smoking-hot griddle until tender and smoky sweet.

Mix all the dressing ingredients together and toss the vegetables in some of the dressing while they are still warm. Serve on a bed of rocket lightly dressed with the rest of the dressing and scattered with the crumbled blue cheese, walnuts and parsley, if using. Devour!

Variation

Char-grilled Jerusalem artichokes are also delectable in a salad of watercress, toasted walnuts and pan-fried pigeon breast with a light red wine vinegar dressing, as a starter or light lunch. Or try them in the spring (see opposite).

Ma's macadamia salad

This is an incredible salad that my mother invented at home. It is bright and colourful, and the creaminess of the toasted macadamia nuts really lifts the dish. It is delicious dressed with the chipotle vinaigrette on page 175, or is just as good with bread and cheese for a simple weekend lunch.

FEEDS 6

2 red onions, halved and cut into wedges

2 red peppers, seeded and cut into chunks

1–2 tablespoons extra virgin olive oil

120g macadamia nuts

½ cucumber, peeled

3 spring onions, finely chopped (see note)

2 shallots, finely chopped

2 heads of chicory, hearts removed and coarsely chopped

½ fennel bulb, diced

1 Braeburn, Granny Smith or other tart green apple, peeled and diced

3 baby gem lettuce, chopped

sea salt and freshly ground black pepper

Preheat the oven to 200°C/400°F/Gas Mark 6.

Toss the onion and red pepper in the olive oil and roast in the oven for 30 minutes. Toast the macadamia nuts in a small roasting tin for 5–7 minutes in the same oven, until they are a lovely caramel colour. Remove the macadamias from the oven and chop coarsely, then set aside to cool while the onion and pepper finish cooking.

Slice the cucumber into quarters lengthways. Now slice down each length, cutting out the seeds (which are watery and would make your salad wishy-washy). Dice the remaining flesh.

To serve, mix all the salad ingredients in a bowl, season with salt and pepper, then toss in the classic French dressing with shallots on page 174.

Note Slice the spring onions in quarters lengthways first so that when you chop them across the width you get lovely finely chopped spring onion.

Bacon and egg salad

I came up with this recipe when I was doing long stints of writing alone at home. I love eating well, but sometimes get lazy and don't want to go through the whole paraphernalia of cooking, especially if it's only me. I know that if I want to keep up my energy level, I need to eat well. This was one of those lunches when I hadn't been shopping so there was not much in the fridge but some rather tired-looking lettuce, an egg and some leftover bacon. I thought about the way egg yolk thickens up the dressing of a Caesar salad and thought I'd try my own bacon and egg salad – the walnuts were thrown in for a bit of added body as I was out of bread, too!

FEEDS 4

10 rashers streaky bacon

1 teaspoon vinegar

1 large Cos or Romaine lettuce or 500g baby spinach leaves

3 spring onions, finely chopped

½ cucumber, seeded and diced (see Ma's macadamia salad opposite for instructions)

80g walnuts, toasted and roughly chopped

1 quantity of classic French dressing with shallots (page 174)

6 eggs

sea salt and freshly ground black pepper

Grill or fry the bacon until crispy, and drain on kitchen paper to absorb any fat. Bring to the boil a saucepan full of water with the vinegar for poaching the eggs. Break up the lettuce into a salad bowl and toss in the spring onion, cucumber and walnuts. Snip the bacon into bits and add to the salad.

When you are ready to eat, dress the salad with the vinaigrette. To poach the eggs, break 3 of them into the pan of simmering water, being careful not to break the yolks. Poach for 2–3 minutes – you want the whites to be just cooked, but the yolks still runny. When the first batch of eggs is ready, fish them out of the water with a slotted spoon and stir them gently into the salad. The joy of this is that it couldn't matter less if your poached eggs are not the perfect shape, as the eggs become part of the dressing itself. Cook the last 3 eggs, this time for a minute longer. Slice into rough chunks and carefully toss into the salad. Season to taste and serve with fresh crusty bread.

Bagna cauda salad

This salad is a take on the classic Italian warm anchovy and garlic sauce from the Piedmont region, which is usually eaten with crudités. The success of the salad depends on the quality of the anchovies you buy. Made with a stale jar of anchovies, it will taste like old socks; try it with some beautiful anchovies stored in extra virgin olive oil and it will be a feast. It makes a lovely autumnal or wintry salad with its robust dressing, proving that summer is not the only time to eat fresh greens. As well as tasting delicious, it looks stunning, with a kaleidoscope of colours on the plate. If you cannot find red chicory, throw in some sliced beetroot (cooked as on page 176) or some thinly shaved pink radishes, to keep the colours alive. This is a quintessential example of something looking good enough to eat.

FEEDS 6

½ head romanesco broccoli (if you can find it) or cauliflower, broken into florets

3 heads red chicory, halved lengthways and cut into thin, wispy slices

4 celery sticks, very finely sliced

4 carrots, peeled and finely shaved with a peeler

2 shallots, finely sliced

1 quantity of bagna cauda dressing (see page 177)

sea salt

1 tablespoon finely chopped fresh flat-leaf parsley (optional)

Steam the broccoli for 5 minutes. Put in a large bowl with the chicory, celery, carrot and shallot. Add the dressing and toss through. Check the seasoning once dressed (it often needs some salt when the salad has been tossed). Scatter with the parsley, if using, and serve. This goes beautifully with the duck on pages 110–11.

Classic bagna cauda

For the classic bagna cauda, melt 8 anchovies in a small saucepan over a low heat with 2 crushed garlic cloves and a knob of butter. Gently stew for a few minutes, then whisk in 25g unsalted butter and 50 ml extra virgin olive oil. Add a splash of red wine vinegar, juice of ½ lemon, and salt and pepper to taste. Serve warm with various crudités (fennel, carrot, celery, artichoke hearts) and steamed baby potatoes for dipping. If you are having a very simple supper dish, grind 3 or 4 walnuts using a mortar and pestle, and mix into the dip with 1 tablespoon freshly grated Parmesan – the perfect simple supper.

Note Don't be upset if the sauce splits – this is quite usual and will not affect the taste.

My kind of fattoush

Fattoush has always been one of my favourite salads, largely because of the delicious dressing which combines garlic with a spice called sumac. I also love the way the deliciously buttery bits of crisp pitta bread meld in with the salad ingredients. I was delighted when I first tried it in a little Lebanese restaurant about 10 years ago. Then Sam and Sam Clarke's amazing book *Moro* came out and included a fattoush. I can't really improve much on their recipe, except that I think you can be quite inventive with what you put in the salad. I love it tossed with feta, to make it into a lunchtime dish, or as a fun starter rather than just a side dish. I also like it with lots of crisp lettuce. I can't always get hold of za'atar, another seasoning that is traditionally used in the dressing, so I have improvised and come up with this alternative. The za'atar is optional.

FEEDS 4

2 pitta breads, split in half
2 tablespoons butter
good pinch of sumac
2 spring onions, finely chopped
2 celery sticks, sliced into thin rounds
300g cauliflower, sliced into slivers
2 baby gem lettuces, chopped
4 carrots, grated
10 radishes, sliced into thin rounds
large handful each of fresh basil, coriander, mint and parsley, roughly chopped
sea salt and freshly ground black pepper

For the dressing

1 teaspoon sesame seed
1 teaspoon cumin seed
1 garlic clove
juice of ½ lemon
1 heaped teaspoon sumac
1 teaspoon za'atar (optional)
½ teaspoon honey
150ml best-quality olive oil

Preheat the oven to 200°C/400°F/Gas Mark 6.

Melt the butter and spread it over the pitta bread. Sprinkle with the sumac, salt and pepper, and toast in the oven for 5-10 minutes until golden – but not black! It burns very easily.

Combine the rest of the salad ingredients in a large salad bowl. To make the dressing, gently warm the sesame and cumin seed in a dry frying pan for 3-4 minutes. Grind up using a mortar and pestle, then mash in the garlic. When you have a smooth paste, slowly add the rest of the dressing ingredients, stirring well to incorporate.

To finish, add the dressing to the salad. Break up the pitta into small, bite-size chunks and add to the salad. Toss through and serve.

Sumac and za'atar

Sumac is a red berry found in the Mediterranean that is dried, then ground to produce an intense red spice that gives food a lemony, slightly sour flavour. Za'atar is another herb found in the Mediterranean and has a flavour a little like thyme. (It is also sometimes sold as a blend of seasonings including the herb, sumac and sesame seeds.) Both sumac and za'atar can be found in good delicatessens, Middle Eastern grocery shops and some supermarkets.

Broad bean salad with mint, lemon zest and goat's cheese

I get thoroughly overexcited every spring at the prospect of broad beans arriving on restaurant menus up and down the country. They do all the fiddly work of shelling the beans and taking off the tough, outer skin of the broad bean to leave the soft, bright green bean inside. I like to do this, too, but it takes a lot of work. Buy the smallest broad beans you can find and the outer skin will be quite soft. Otherwise, relax in front of a good movie and get shelling, enjoying the fact that the season is short, or use frozen baby broad beans, which are generally an excellent quality.

FEEDS 6

650g baby broad beans, fresh or frozen

½ cucumber, peeled, seeded and diced

2 celery sticks, diced

handful of chopped fresh mint

grated zest of 1 lemon

100g goat's cheese

1 quantity of classic French dressing with shallots (see page 174)

1 garlic clove, crushed

Cook the broad beans in boiling salted water until they are tender, about 10 minutes. Drain and rinse in cold water to refresh. At this point, you can slip the broad beans out of their coats. (I find it quite a therapeutic job, but, if you can't face it, do make sure you are using small, tender beans.) Gently mix together in a large salad bowl with the cucumber, celery, mint and lemon zest. Break up the goat's cheese into small pieces and sprinkle into the salad.

Whisk the French dressing with the crushed garlic so that it is well mixed. Pour over the salad and carefully toss, trying not to break up the goat's cheese too much.

Pan-fried manchego, watercress and Serrano ham with ripe figs

This is inspired by a starter I once had at Assaggi in Notting Hill. The secret is to leave the young manchego out to dry a little, then fry in a very hot non-stick pan, letting it form a crust before you turn it. Make it ahead of time so you don't have to do this bit in front of guests. The dish is completed with a drizzling of the very best extra virgin olive oil: a new, grassy, fiery one is best. This is quite filling, so it could even do for a light lunch.

FEEDS 4 HUNGRY PEOPLE

250g young, firm manchego cheese, rind sliced off

olive oil for frying

12 slices Serrano ham or chorizo or Parma ham

8 very ripe figs

best-quality extra virgin olive oil

a little saba (see note on page 167) or reduced balsamic vinegar (see page 80)

200g watercress or wild rocket

grated zest and juice of 1 lemon

sea salt and freshly ground black pepper

Cut the manchego into 1–1½cm slices. Make sure there are enough so that everyone gets an equal number of slices. Leave to dry out in the air for at least an hour (preferably 2–3).

Heat a heavy, non-stick frying pan until extremely hot. Pour in a dribble of olive oil – just enough to coat the pan. Carefully slide in the cheese slices, cooking them in 2 or 3 batches. Fry for 30–60 seconds a side until they become brown and crispy. It is important here to allow time to form a crispy crust on the cheese's surface, but not to leave the cheese in the pan long enough for it to melt altogether. Have two spatulas to hand so that you can better turn and remove the cheese slices. When they are done, transfer to a plate to firm up again.

Arrange the Serrano ham in a high, folded pile on one side of each plate. Make two slits across the top of the figs in a cross pattern, and pinch the bottom of the figs so that they open out like flowers. Sprinkle each one with a little extra virgin olive oil, a few drops of saba and some salt and pepper. Arrange the figs opposite to the ham on each plate.

Toss the watercress with sea salt, pepper, a squeeze of lemon juice and extra virgin olive oil. You want the leaves to be glistening, but not drenched. Arrange a small pile of watercress on a third side of each plate and the slices of manchego on the fourth (you will end up with a 'square' of piles). Alternatively, arrange the whole lot on a large platter for people to help themselves. This mixture is also delicious tossed in freshly cooked al dente pasta.

Puddings and chocolate

Despite trying to eat healthily 80 per cent of the time, I am always let down by my sweet tooth, which has been developing at a steady rate over the years. While I may not always go for puddings in restaurants (having already overdone myself on preceding courses), puddings are still an important part of a meal. Weekend eating would not be complete without something sweet at the end of lunch, whether it's a simple summer fruit dish, a more seductive tart or just an innocent piece of dark chocolate truffle. I love to have puddings at around tea-time, when you have reached that funny time of day when you are tempted to start eating, even though supper is fast approaching.

Puddings can be works of art that take up entire afternoons. Half the fun is in the anticipation and it is always a thrill to see people's faces lighting up at some wicked indulgence. Puddings really are just that – indulgent treats. You wouldn't want to eat them every day, but when you do give in to them you should do so with gleeful abandon.

Some puddings can be whizzed up in no time at all. My seven-day ice cream is fixed for just such a time. Maybe you have lots of friends coming round for supper but are late back from work and feeling harassed. Splash out on a beautiful shop-bought vanilla ice cream and pull together the sauce as your guests are chatting at the table after the main course. The chocolate toast on page 212 is similarly easy. It can be as relaxed and quick as that, but still a treat for all concerned.

Chocolate is another thing altogether. I cannot begin to imagine life without chocolate. What I really go for is the rich dark chocolate that fills you with a warm, euphoric buzz, like sipping a cold whisky in a piping-hot bath. For this type of fix I buy chocolate with a minimum of 70 per cent cocoa solids. Anything less and you're in danger of compromising on quality. Very occasionally 70 per cent is too rich and dark for a recipe, in which case buy a chocolate with a lower cocoa content, but still get the best that you can afford. Valhrona chocolate is first-rate, as is Green and Black's cooking chocolate – both use fair-trade beans. If you are a milk chocolate kind of person, then tuck into the Mars Bar sauce on page 212–13, but I bet it doesn't grab you as much as the chocolate ganache tart on page 214. Try it and see.

Custard

Custard is the basis of so many delicious puddings. Not only does it make ice cream (of which more later), but it also can be used to make other favourites such as old-fashioned trifle (a pudding not to be sniffed at) and bread and butter pudding. Pour it over jam tarts, summer puddings, stewed fruit, treacle puddings, not to mention the odd bowl of corn flakes. Custards can be baked for my favourite, crème brûlée, or as per the rhubarb and custard recipe on page 194, or they can be used to fill tarts (see below). They can be flavoured with the classic vanilla (use 2 or 3 pods to flavour a standard recipe if you are feeling decadent), with a subtly Moorish cardamom pod or with the more unusual star anise. Explore further with citrus juices, coffee and chocolate – the sky is the limit. The difference between a home-made custard and a bought one is huge. Custards are extremely good flavoured with liqueurs, too, but be careful as too much alcohol will separate the mixture.

MAKES ABOUT 650ML

600ml full-fat milk or 50:50 milk and double cream (you will need cream if you are making ice cream)

1 vanilla pod, split lengthways

6 egg yolks

50g caster sugar

Heat the milk to scalding point and add the vanilla pod. Remove from the heat, scrape out the vanilla seeds into the custard with the blade of a knife (discard the pod) and leave to infuse for 20–25 minutes. Whisk the egg yolks with the sugar. Once infused, beat the cream mixture into the eggs yolks, whisking all the time. Return to the pan and cook over a low heat, stirring constantly with a wooden spoon. This can take as little as 10 minutes, but up to 30 minutes if you cook it very slowly. If you cook it fast, have a bowl of iced water nearby so that you can plunge the saucepan in it if the egg looks in danger of scrambling. If this happens, whisk the mixture vigorously until it cools a little. You want to get the consistency of smooth double cream. Strain and serve.

Cardamom custard

This custard is delicious with rhubarb, whether poached, crumbled, trifled or souffléed. Add ½ teaspoon green cardamom seeds to the milk in place of the vanilla pod, and proceed with the basic custard recipe.

Mini custard tarts

Try making some of these custard tarts when you have some free time. You can make lots of shortcrust pastry tartlets using the pastry recipe on page 64, perfect if you want to churn out masses of sweet or savoury tarts for a party.

Mini anise custard tarts with boozy figs

Follow the instructions for the fig anise tart on pages 198–9, infusing the custard with orange zest and star anise, and slicing figs that have been soaked in hot brandy into each tartlet.

Mini brandied custard tarts with marron glacé

Make the brandy cream from page 208, using the best-quality brandy or dark rum you can afford. Fill the tart cases with the cream and decorate with slithers of marron glacé (and gratings of chocolate if you really want to gild the lily). Great for Christmas parties.

Mini lemon custard tarts

I love lemon custard. It's one of my favourite tart fillings, made famous by the River Café. Zest and juice 5 lemons and put them in a heavy-bottomed saucepan with 230g caster sugar, 4 whole eggs and 6 egg yolks. Whisk until the eggs are broken up. Continue whisking, gradually adding 100g softened unsalted butter. The mixture will thicken and start coating the back of a wooden spoon. Continue adding a further 100g butter, whisking all the time. Fill the tart cases and bake for 3–4 minutes at 230°C/450°F/Gas Mark 8.

Rhubarb and custard

This was inspired by an incredible lunch I had at Petersham Nursery when the legendary Maggie Beer was visiting from Australia, giving a workshop on verjuice. The custard is just like a crème brûlée base, so, if you feel like the classic crème brûlée, substitute the orange juice for a vanilla pod and add a slug of your favourite liqueur to the cream. Sprinkle with caster sugar when cold and grill to get the burnt sugar topping, then refrigerate. This orange version is stunning with blood oranges, in season from January to March.

FEEDS 8

7 large rhubarb stalks, cut into 2cm lengths

1 vanilla pod, split lengthways and seeds scraped out

4 tablespoons caster sugar (or more to taste)

For the orange custard

juice of 6 oranges and grated zest of 3

100ml verjuice (see page 130)

110g sugar

1 tablespoon Grand Marnier

600ml double cream

2 eggs

4 egg yolks

Preheat the oven to 170°C/340°F/Gas Mark 3–4.

To make the orange custard, put the orange juice and zest in a pan with the verjuice and sugar, and simmer until reduced to a rich caramel syrup. Stir in the Grand Marnier and cream, and remove from the heat.

Whisk the eggs and yolks in a bowl until light and fluffy, then whisk into the caramel syrup. Strain through a fine sieve and pour into a 1-litre soufflé dish. Stand the dish in a baking dish filled with water and bake in the oven for 40–45 minutes until set, checking that it is not overcooking and scrambling towards the end of the cooking time. It should be just set and still wobble a bit when gently shaken. Cool and refrigerate.

To poach the rhubarb, put the rhubarb into a saucepan with the vanilla seeds and add a splash of water. Poach over a low heat for about 20 minutes, until the rhubarb is soft but not collapsed. Add the sugar to taste, bearing in mind that it is nice to meld a tart rhubarb with the sweet custard.

Serve spoonfuls of the orange custard with the bright pink rhubarb and syrup. Alternatively, bake the custard in mini soufflé dishes for individual helpings.

Baked orange tart

Follow the method above until the point before baking the orange custard in the oven, then pour it into a blind-baked tart case (page 198). Bake in the oven at 170°C/340°F/Gas Mark 3–4 for 20–25 minutes, then leave the tart in the turned-off oven to cool, to prevent cracking. Delicious with cream.

The easiest lemon pudding

This is a winner for those times that invariably arrive, spring, summer, autumn or winter, when you have asked lots of people over the next day and just can't face the thought of even going into the kitchen, let alone cooking. It takes no time to make and is fairly addictive.

FEEDS 6

120g caster sugar

grated zest and juice of 2 lemons plus 1 tablespoon freshly squeezed lemon juice

1 wine glass of dry white wine

570ml double cream, softly whipped

1 quantity of almond praline (see page 205)

Whip the caster sugar, lemon juice and zest, and white wine into the cream, being careful not to overbeat or you will make butter. Chill in wine glasses or small water glasses until ready to serve. Meanwhile, make the praline as given on page 205. When set, break up with a rolling pin and sprinkle over the syllabub.

Alternatively, serve the syllabub with mixed summer berries or cinnamon-spiced poached fruits. We like poached apples, pears or quinces in the autumn and winter.

Poaching

Poaching is the easiest and most delicious way to cook many different kinds of food. Poaching pears, apples, quinces and rhubarb will allow you to make jams, fools, tarts, purées, soufflés and other amazing puddings and give them a lovely scent. Simply put equal quantities of sugar and water in a pan and heat to melt the sugar. Add 1–2 vanilla pods split down the length with a knife, 1 bay leaf and some lemon zest (grated or in strips). Add your fruit and simmer until soft, turning halfway through if the fruit is not covered in the poaching liquid.

Poach chicken or salmon by covering with water and adding bay leaves, black peppercorns, celery, carrot and onion to the poaching liquid. Bring to the boil and simmer gently for 5 minutes. Turn off the heat and leave the meat to cool in the liquid, keeping all the juicy goodness inside the flesh. A delicate and healthy way to eat.

How to poach an egg? See page 54.

Pear and almond tart

By all means cheat with the pastry and buy ready-made (it can be really good), but I rather like making it and it takes no time at all. The secret is to do the pastry first, and fast, in the food processor, and to handle it as little as possible. Follow the method for the pissaladière on pages 64–5 and the tips at right and you should have no trouble.

FEEDS 6–8

For the pastry

250g plain flour
25g icing or caster sugar
125g butter
2 egg yolks

For the frangipane

175g almonds, whole or ready ground
175g sugar
175g butter
1 egg plus 1 yolk

For the pears

200g caster sugar
1 vanilla pod, split lengthways
1 bay leaf
grated zest of 1 lemon
5 comice pears, peeled, cored and cut into quarters
1 punnet blackberries (optional)
dash of brandy (optional)

Follow the pastry instructions on page 64, whizzing the egg into the pastry first, then adding splashes of water if you need it to pull the pastry together. Chill the pastry in the refrigerator for at least 30 minutes, then roll out to fit a 24cm pie dish. Bake the pastry shell blind in a preheated 180°C/350°F/Gas Mark 4 oven and leave to cool.

If using whole almonds, heat in the oven for 5 minutes to bring out the flavour, then grind in a food processor (or using a mortar and pestle). When they are very finely ground, add the butter and sugar, whizz briefly, then add the egg. Combine and set the frangipane mixture aside.

To poach the pears, bring 200ml water to the boil in a saucepan and add the sugar. Simmer until the sugar has dissolved, then add the vanilla pod, bay leaf and lemon zest. Add the pears and poach for 10 minutes, then drain and slice thinly, discarding the poaching liquid.

Spread the frangipane over the base of the pastry case and arrange the pears on top in overlapping fans. Sprinkle with blackberries (if using) and a dash of brandy (if you are feeling extravagant). Bake for 25–30 minutes until puffed up, golden and beautiful-looking.

Fig anise custard tart

This pudding was the result of having some friends over for lunch and at the last minute suddenly deciding they did need a pudding after all. The figs were waiting in the cupboard (not sure how long they had been lurking).

Fill your pastry case with 10 dried figs which you have halved across the middle and simmered in a sugar syrup (75ml water and 75ml any anise-flavoured liqueur such as as Sambuca mixed with 160g sugar) for 15 minutes. Cover the figs with the custard on page 000, which you have infused with the zest of 1 orange and 2 star anise in place of the vanilla pod. Bake in a preheated oven at 160°C/325°F/Gas Mark 3 for 10–15 minutes until golden. Serve with the leftover syrup and Greek yoghurt or crème fraîche. The figs will have risen splendidly to the top of the tart.

Pears and chocolate sauce

Poach the pears as in the main recipe, peeling them but leaving them whole. Serve with the chocolate sauce on page 212 laced with a tablespoon of brandy or rum – delicious.

For mini tarts

Silicon sheets with mini tart moulds are available in all good kitchen shops. Make double the quantity of pastry in the recipe above and cut out small circles, allowing a good 2cm extra width to allow for shrinkage and fitting the pastry down into the tartlet moulds. Prick the tart cases and put one silicon sheet on top of each set of pastry cases in place of baking beans so that the tart cases stay flat. Freeze for 10–15 minutes before baking to reduce shrinkage. These tarts can make mini pissaladières (see pages 64–5), mini custard tarts (page 193), mini lemon custard tarts (page 193) or mini wild mushroom tarts (use the filling from page 144). Get experimenting!

Making pastry

People are inclined to let memory override reason, only ever recalling failed pastry-making attempts. Practised once or twice, however, pastry is easy. Ensure the butter is as cold as possible. You then need 5 minutes with a food processor, 30 minutes while it rests in the fridge (and you get on with everything else), 5 minutes with a rolling pin, and 15 minutes in the freezer before baking. What could be simpler? Make some and freeze it for a rainy day, then whip it out to prepare something good in moments.

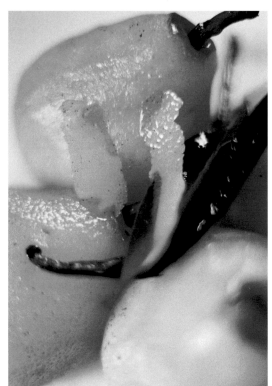

Prune tarte Tatin with Armagnac cream

Together, prunes and Armagnac form one of my favourite food combinations –
a real match made in heaven. If you don't feel like making this pudding, just
blend the soaked prunes with custard and make an ice cream laced with
Armagnac and it will be wonderful. This pudding is delicious though, and not
very much effort, as the pastry is bought ready-made (do make sure you buy
a good-quality pastry, one made with butter rather than other fats). I was
experimenting with frangipane recipes when I discovered a hazelnut butter in
Maggie Beer's beautiful cookbook *Maggie's Table*. The hazelnuts give the
sweet butter a lovely rich flavour.

FEEDS 6–8

For the tart

400g prunes

60ml good-quality cooking brandy
or Armagnac

250ml red wine

1 vanilla pod, split lengthways

1 tablespoon caster sugar

1 sheet good-quality ready-made
puff pastry

a little beaten egg and milk, for the
egg wash

For the nut butter

100g caster sugar

2 large egg yolks

110g unsalted butter, softened

100g hazelnuts, roasted and finely
ground

For the Armagnac cream

2 egg yolks

2 tablespoons caster sugar

60ml Armagnac

300ml double cream, whipped

Preheat the oven to 200°C/400°F/Gas Mark 6. You will need an
18cm cake tin or baking dish.

Simmer the prunes, brandy, wine, vanilla pod and caster
sugar until the prunes are soft and juicy, about 25 minutes.
Most of the liquid will have been absorbed.

While the prunes are simmering, make the nut butter. Put
half the sugar and 1 tablespoon water in a small pan and
simmer until it has turned a good caramel colour (see page
206). Add another 75ml water, watching out for spitting. Using
an electric mixer, beat the rest of the sugar and the egg yolks
together until light and fluffy. With the beater still on, gradually
mix in the syrup, then the butter, a bit at a time. Finally add the
ground hazelnuts. Arrange the prunes in the cake tin or baking
dish and spoon over the nut butter. Be generous with this – it
gives the most amazing flavour to the prunes. Place the rolled
puff pastry over the prunes, tucking the overhanging pastry
into the sides of the dish. Brush the pastry with the egg wash.
Bake in the oven until puffed and golden, about 30 minutes.

To make the Armagnac cream, whisk the yolks and sugar
until light and fluffy (about 3 minutes), then beat in the
Armagnac. Fold in the double cream. This cream will not stand
for more than an hour or two, so it is not advisable to make it
too long in advance. Serve the tart in its dish or upturned, as is
traditional, with generous helpings of the Armagnac cream.

Blackberry and stem ginger pudding

We were playing around with sticky steamed puddings at Petersham. I used to think that you needed to steam puddings in bain-maries, and get fiddly with string and greaseproof paper, but actually this is just like steamed pudding minus the suet. I like to take it out of the oven when it is still slightly gooey in the middle, so you can spoon dollops onto someone's plate and serve with the syrup and lashings of softly whipped cream.

FEEDS 8–10 (DEPENDING ON GREED)

200g unsalted butter
120g caster sugar
4 eggs
100g self-raising flour
50g ground almonds
1 teaspoon baking powder
100g stem ginger, finely chopped
finely grated zest of 1 lemon
300g golden syrup
200g blackberries
softly whipped double cream to serve

For the warm syrup sauce

1 x 300g tin golden syrup
40g stem ginger, finely chopped
zest and juice of 1 lemon

Butter a 22cm round cake tin and dust with flour. Preheat the oven to 180°C/350°F/Gas Mark 4.

Cream the butter and sugar until very pale, light and fluffy (5–10 minutes in an electric mixer). Add the eggs one by one, beating in between each addition. Fold in the flour, almonds (it is better if you have the time to toast whole, blanched almonds and grind them yourself) and baking powder. Fold in the ginger and lemon zest.

Pour the golden syrup into the tin and scatter with the blackberries. Pour the cake mixture over the blackberries and bake for 25–30 minutes until springy to the touch. It is nice to just undercook it and have a gooey pudding.

To make the warm syrup sauce, gently heat the golden syrup, ginger, lemon zest and juice together. Serve the pudding with the double cream and the warm sauce poured over.

Variations

- Use whatever berries are in season to create your own sticky pudding . . . raspberries are delicious with lemon zest, as are blueberries and white chocolate chips.
- Try 1 tablespoon cocoa powder in place of the ginger in the pudding mixture and serve chocolate sauce (page 000) with 60g chopped toasted hazelnuts in place of the syrup sauce.
- Use the zest and juice of 2 oranges in place of the ginger in the pudding mixture and 300g dark Seville marmalade topped with thin slices of 1 orange spread on the bottom instead of golden syrup. Mix the juice and zest of another orange into your syrup for the sauce.

Gooseberry fool

A good fool is the perfect way to enjoy summer or winter fruits. Whether it's a prune fool in the depths of winter, apple fool throughout autumn and beyond or seasonal fools in the height of summer, this nursery school way of eating has an eternal appeal. My mother always adds a little beaten egg white to the mix to lighten the pudding, but otherwise it's just a matter of a little poaching and spoonfuls of softly whipped cream. Yum!

FEEDS 6–8 HAPPILY

450g gooseberries
150–200ml sugar to taste
finely grated zest and juice of 1 orange
1 vanilla pod, split lengthways
1 tablespoon Pernod or Muscat
300ml double cream, softly whipped
3 egg whites (optional)

Put the gooseberries, sugar, orange zest and juice into a heavy saucepan. Scrape the vanilla seeds into the pan, then simmer gently with a lid on for about 15 minutes. Push the mixture through a fine sieve to separate the gooseberries' tops and tails from the purée. Stir in the Pernod and blend the gooseberry purée until it is fairly smooth.

Taste the gooseberries for tartness, adding more sugar if necessary, then gently fold in the softly whipped cream so the two are half-mixed like a ripple. The fool should be floppy, relaxed and delicious served in little glasses or glass bowls with toasted flaked almonds or sticks of buttery shortbread.

If you are using the egg whites, beat them in a metallic bowl until they form stiff peaks and fold into the mixture. Pour into serving glasses or one big bowl, and chill until serving. This will result in a fool that holds its shape more and is a little lighter.

Variations

Try this recipe with every fruit under the sun. My favourites are rhubarb fool with halved English seasonal strawberries folded through, or apple and quince fool in the winter.

Gooseberry granita

This fool can easily be turned into an elegant granita for a dinner-party pudding. Make as for the gooseberry purée, adding more sugar as freezing will make it tarter, and transfer to a flattish container. Freeze for 3–4 hours, stirring with a fork after an hour to get a rough granita texture.

Summer pudding nougat ice cream

This pudding, which I adapted from Stephanie Alexander's *Cook's Companion*, is utterly delicious. It is like the summer pudding that my grandfather used to make for me, but stirred into a nougat ice cream. By all means use frozen berries if you get a yearning for this out of season. The ice cream is also great with rhubarb purée, but try it with quince, which has a delicate, flowery flavour, or sharp gooseberry, which cuts through the sweetness.

FEEDS 10

For the summer fruits

300g mixed raspberries, redcurrants, blackcurrants, strawberries

1 vanilla pod, split lengthways

zest of 1 lemon

caster sugar to taste

1 good tablespoon Cointreau (optional)

For the almond praline

120g caster sugar

90g flaked almonds, toasted

For the ice cream

80g caster sugar

45g liquid glucose

60g honey

6 egg whites

600ml double cream, softly whipped

You will need a sugar thermometer, an electric whisk and a bowl filled with ice

First make the summer fruit purée. Poach the berries with a splash of water, the vanilla pod, lemon zest and sugar for 15 minutes until soft. Purée, sieve and stir in the Cointreau, if using, and a tablespoon of the whipped double cream. Set aside.

Next make the praline. Put the sugar in a heavy saucepan and pour over just enough water to cover. Dissolve the sugar over a medium heat, brushing the sides of the pan with cold water to prevent crystals forming. As the caramel starts turning golden, swirl it around to distribute it without stirring. When the caramel is golden all over, pour onto a baking sheet over the almonds. When it is set, break up using a mortar and pestle, or roll with a rolling pin. You can do this in the food processor, but you will get a much more powdered result with fewer caramelised nut chunks, which are delicious in the ice cream.

For the ice cream, dissolve the sugar, glucose and honey over a medium heat in the same pan you used to make the praline. When the mixture is fully dissolved, heat it to the soft-ball stage (116°C/240°F) on a sugar thermometer – it will bubble vigorously, but do not be put off by this. Remove from the heat and beat the egg whites in large metal bowl until they form stiff peaks. Place the egg-white bowl into the bowl of ice and beat in the syrup until the mixture has cooled to room temperature. Slowly fold in the cream until thoroughly combined. Fold in the praline. Gently swirl half the fruit purée into the nougat, creating a ripple effect. Pour into a container or terrine mould, cover with clingfilm or greaseproof paper, and freeze for at least 12 hours. Serve in slices with the rest of the berry sauce.

Monday–Sunday vanilla ice cream

Nothing beats a really good-quality vanilla ice cream, especially if you are topping it with delicious nuts or gooey sticky sauces. Making your own ice cream is easy if you have an ice-cream machine. Just take the custard recipe on page 192 and churn it up. Buying a good-quality ice cream is the next best thing, but you do have to cough up for the very best quality. Even brands of ice cream labelled with words such as 'real Cornish cream ice cream' turn out to be full of hydrogenated fats and skimmed milk powder. Read the label and opt for top-notch brands that contain eggs, cream and real vanilla. That way you will really be doing justice to your sauces and serving a first-class minimum-work pudding for your friends. Below are seven classic vanilla ice-cream toppings that will keep you happy throughout the week. The almond praline on page 205 also makes a delicious topping.

Caramel sauce

200g sugar

60ml double cream

1 tablespoon of your favourite liqueur (Cointreau, Armagnac, whisky liqueur etc.)

Go for broke by serving this sauce with pieces of caramelised banana, pineapple, pear, apple, peach etc. fried in a bit of butter, sprinkled with sugar when still in the pan and turning golden, then flambéed with whatever liqueur you are using.

Put the sugar in a heavy saucepan over a medium-high heat and just cover it with water. Let the sugar dissolve and the syrup start bubbling, and slowly it will start turning a golden caramel colour. Do *not* stir. Swish the pan around so that the caramelising syrup is evenly dispersed. It will soon start turning a dark brown colour. You need to wait until this caramel is right on the edge of turning black so that the bitter caramel flavour offsets the sweetness of the sugar, giving a glorious, complex flavour. You can tell when it is about to start burning, as the syrup begins to smoke and turn really dark. At this point, swirl the caramel again, remove from the heat and pop in the cream and booze quickly, which will arrest the cooking, taking extra care not to get splashed as the caramel will bubble up furiously. Swirl around and finally stir. Serve with ice cream.

Crème brûlée ice cream

Follow the recipe above (without the cream and liqueur), but pour the caramel out onto a greased baking sheet when it has turned dark golden brown. Leave to set, then break up into shards with a rolling pin. Serve stirred into or decorating vanilla ice cream.

Chocolate sauce

See page 212. Make at least double the amount you think you'll need so that you can eat chocolate sauce with ice cream, rather than the other way round.

Affogato

Alex Garcia, my favourite girl in Mexico City, got me onto this Italian classic. Simply pour rich, strong espresso over best-quality vanilla ice cream. It provides the perfect sugar and caffeine hit after a big lunch and is also great fun to serve to people in individual espresso cups (which we collect in my flat).

Pedro Ximenez sherry sauce

Dark, syrupy sherry and vanilla ice cream create alternating coffee and chocolate flavours on your tongue. Either pour the sherry straight onto the ice cream or reduce 200ml by half for a rich syrup. Swirl into vanilla ice cream and serve.

Meringue ice cream

Follow the basic hazelnut meringue recipe on page 208 and crunch up into vanilla ice cream. Even easier, buy in both the ice cream and the meringue, and make a delicious crunchy pudding.

Prunes and Armagnac

Poach the prunes as on page 202, adding 100g sugar and a split vanilla pod to the poaching liquid. Whizz the prunes for 5–10 seconds in a food processor, and serve mixed through vanilla ice cream with extra Armagnac poured over the top.

Winter hazelnut meringue cake with chestnut brandy cream

This is a fun, gooey pudding to make for a big family party, whether you are opting for the winter chestnut version with blackberries and marron purée, or the summer one with fresh raspberries and lemon curd (pictured). It is not the most sophisticated cake in the world, but it tastes incredible and looks good enough to dive into. The perfect cake to make for a special occasion.

FEEDS 10 HAPPILY

8 egg whites

pinch of salt

500g unrefined caster sugar (see note)

4 teaspoons cornflour

2 teaspoons white wine vinegar

½ teaspoon vanilla extract

150g hazelnuts, toasted and roughly chopped

For the filling

2 x 435g tins marron purée

4 tablespoons brandy

100g caster sugar

900ml double cream, softly whipped

250g blackberries

marron glacé (optional)

Preheat the oven to 180°C/350°F/Gas Mark 4.

Whisk the egg whites with a pinch of salt until they form stiff peaks. Gradually add the sugar, a third at a time, letting the egg whites form smooth, satiny peaks between each addition. Sprinkle over the cornflour, white wine vinegar and vanilla extract, and beat in slowly. Fold in the cooled hazelnuts.

Line two baking sheets with greaseproof paper. Spread the meringue mixture into a circle or oblong on each sheet, making one slightly larger than the other, which will become the bottom of your meringue cake. Put in the oven and reduce the oven temperature to 130°C/265°C/Gas Mark 1. Bake for 50–60 minutes, until crisp, then turn the oven off, letting the meringue cool completely in the oven (this is brilliant to do just before going to bed if you are planning to eat the cake the next day, and ensures a squidgy middle to the meringue).

When you are ready for pudding, turn out the marron purée into a bowl and whisk vigorously to a smooth paste. Whisk in the brandy and sugar, and, when you have a smooth purée, fold in one-third of the cream.

Place the larger meringue on a plate and spread with the double cream and half the marron brandy cream. Scatter with half the blackberries. Place the second meringue on top and spread with the remaining marron brandy cream. Decorate with the remaining blackberries and slices of marron glacé, if you like.

Note Do use unrefined caster sugar to get a lovely ivory shade to the meringue.

Summer raspberry and lemon meringue cake
To make the summer variation pictured here, in place of the marron filling, fold two-thirds of the double cream with a small pot of good-quality lemon curd (or make your own). Use this as a filling and top the meringue cake with the remaining whipped cream, a large punnet of summer raspberries and a few extra chopped toasted hazelnuts.

Chilli chocolate truffles

These truffles are easiest to make in big batches and store in the freezer until you need them, though beware of leaving them lying around – they are dangerously moreish. My flatmate Joe and I find it all too easy to nab one whenever we walk past. They are the perfect way to end dinner – not quite a pudding, but nonetheless a lovely chocolate fix. They are brilliant for packing into boxes and giving as presents to friends. Devilishly good. If you're not a chilli fan, omit the chilli flakes for subtly spiced chocolate.

FEEDS MANY

500g dark chocolate
(70% cocoa solids)

200g dark chocolate
(50% cocoa solids)

good pinch of allspice

good pinch of ground cinnamon

10 cloves

1 teaspoon dried chilli flakes

400ml double cream

30g butter

2 tablespoons dark rum or whisky
or brandy

50g cocoa powder

Grease a 30 x 12cm (or thereabouts) baking tin with a little vegetable oil and line the tin with clingfilm.

Grind the allspice, cinnamon, cloves and chilli using a mortar and pestle. Gently heat the double cream and the ground spices in a heavy-bottomed pan. When hot but not boiling, add to the chocolate in a bowl and stir through. (It is very important that the cream does not boil because if you scald the chocolate with too hot a cream you will have to throw everything away and start again.) If the chocolate has not melted completely, suspend your bowl over a pan of simmering water to warm the chocolate gently and melt any last chunks. Stir in the butter and rum. Pour the chocolate mixture into the tin, ensuring the top is level and the mixture has filled the corners. Freeze for an hour.

To finish, sift the cocoa powder into a large bowl. Remove the chocolate from the freezer and carefully turn out onto a chopping board. Peel back the clingfilm and cut into 2–3cm cubes, then toss gently in the cocoa powder. Store in a plastic bag in the freezer until you want to use them.

Note If you use all 70 per cent cocoa solids chocolate to make these truffles you will need to add 1 tablespoon golden syrup to the mixture, or the chocolate will be too rich and bitter.

For a mellower truffle, omit the chilli for a lovely spiced chocolate flavour.

Chocolate toast

This is quite possibly the easiest and most wicked 'pudding' I have come across. The recipe is thanks to Henrietta Thewes, an exceptionally good cook who lives in Perthshire and is, like me, a great fan of Catalan flavours.

FEEDS 2

4 slices of sourdough bread (can be stale)

4 tablespoons very good extra virgin olive oil

150–200g very good dark chocolate (at least 70% cocoa solids), broken into chunks

Maldon sea salt

Toast the bread on both sides under a grill or in the oven at about 180°C/350°F/Gas Mark 4. Drizzle over the olive oil and top with the bits of chocolate. Place under the grill or back in the oven again until the chocolate has melted. Sprinkle with sea salt and tuck in.

Chocolate sauce

A rich, dark chocolate sauce poured over the best vanilla ice cream (bought or home-made) makes an utterly delicious pudding. The sauce takes five minutes. I think this is one of the simplest, most delicious treats you can give to friends. It is so rarely done, but is always a hit.

FEEDS AT LEAST 4 VERY GREEDY PEOPLE, IF NOT MORE

250g dark chocolate (70% cocoa solids), preferably Valhrona, roughly grated or broken into small pieces

30g butter

1 tablespoon golden syrup

4 tablespoons cream

50–60ml milk

1 tablespoon cognac, dark rum or whisky (optional)

Put a saucepan half-filled with water on to simmer. When it is simmering, put a heatproof bowl on top of the saucepan, being careful that the bottom doesn't touch the water. Melt the chocolate in the bowl, making sure that the water never boils too much but just gently warms the chocolate. Stir in the rest of the ingredients and, if you're feeling wicked, add a splash of a spirit to give your sauce some character (cognac if you're putting it on pears; dark rum or whisky is great with ice cream; Cointreau is a winner if you love Terry's chocolate orange). Once the sauce is smooth, use it to top whatever takes your fancy. It keeps for at least a week covered in the refrigerator.

Toblerone or Mars Bar sauce

This is also delicious on ice cream, but is a sweeter variation on the dark chocolate sauce above. Break 200g Toblerone or Mars

Bars and 100g dark chocolate into chunks. Melt over a low heat with 60ml full-fat milk and a knob of butter. Serve poured over your favourite vanilla ice cream. Feeds 6–8.

Tommi's tip

Good-quality chocolate burns very easily, so either melt it gradually in a microwave, stirring in between blasts of heat, or make a bain-marie by using a heatproof bowl set over a pan of simmering water. Always make sure the water doesn't touch the bottom of the bowl. You want the bowl to be gently heated by the water's steam, rather than the scalding water, which would scorch the chocolate.

Chocolate ganache tart

This recipe is much like a giant chocolate truffle. It takes no time to prepare if you have an electric whisk and can be quickly put together the day before or the morning of an evening party, then left in the refrigerator to chill well and free the oven up for cooking other things. The important thing to watch for is that your oven is on a low setting. The tart should never 'rise' too much or you will lose the beautiful, velvety texture. Have faith, cook it on low and when it comes out of the oven it will still wobble gently in the middle. Once it cools and sets in the refrigerator it will slice beautifully.

Served with plenty of double cream and maybe some seasonal berries (strawberries in early summer, raspberries in late summer, blackberries in autumn), this tart makes a beautifully elegant and sinfully good pudding. The vanilla pod is an extravagance, but gives a lovely rounded taste.

FEEDS 8 VERY COMFORTABLY

175g caster sugar

6 egg yolks

565ml double cream

1 vanilla pod, halved lengthways

285g dark chocolate (70% cocoa solids), preferably Valhrona, roughly grated or chopped into small pieces

Preheat the oven to 120°C/250°F/Gas Mark ½. Grease a 28cm loose-bottomed tart tin with butter.

Whisk the sugar and egg yolks together until they have tripled in volume and look light and fluffy. Heat the cream with the vanilla pod in a bowl over a pan of simmering water (making sure the bottom of the bowl doesn't touch the water). When the cream is hot, scrape out the vanilla seeds into the cream and discard the pod. Add the chocolate, stirring with a wooden spoon until melted.

Carefully fold half the chocolate mixture into the eggs to keep the light, fluffy texture. Fold this mixture back into the remaining chocolate. Pour the mixture into your prepared tin and place on a baking sheet in the oven for 1 hour. (The cake will still be soft and slightly wobbly when cooked, but will firm up when it cools.) Remove from the oven and allow to cool, then chill in the refrigerator for 1 hour before serving.

Note If the tart starts to rise, the oven is too hot. It should remain level in the tin throughout cooking to ensure a velvety texture. When it is cooked it will look just a little puffed up.

Variation

Try flavouring the chocolate mixture with the ground seeds
of 3 cardamom pods and serve with a teaspoon of marmalade.
The pudding is also great cooked in individual ramekins or in
a pastry case (see page 198) for a gloriously rich chocolate tart.

The best chocolate cake . . .

This chocolate cake has been in my repertoire since I was eight. I got it from a lovely French woman who brought it to the picnic where I met her. The cake is rich and dense, with a fudge-like consistency. I persuaded her to give me the recipe and I have been making it ever since. It takes me about 10 minutes from the first chocolate melt to getting it in the oven – perfect for whipping out on a lazy weekend or for a birthday treat. It also makes extremely good brownies when cooked in a rectangular tin.

FEEDS 8-10

190g dark chocolate (70% cocoa solids), preferably Valhrona, roughly grated or chopped into small pieces

190g unsalted butter, roughly cubed

190g caster sugar

pinch of salt

pinch of ground cinnamon

100g plain flour

3 medium eggs

Preheat the oven to 170°C/340°F/Gas Mark 3–4. Lightly grease a 19cm cake tin with butter.

Melt the chocolate and butter together in a large bowl, either in a bain-marie or a bowl over a pan of simmering water (see page 214) or in a microwave, stirring between blasts. When smooth, beat in the sugar, salt and cinnamon using a wooden spoon. Sift in the flour bit by bit, stirring between sifts. Beat the eggs in a separate bowl, then add to the chocolate mixture. Pour into the prepared tin and bake in the oven for 40 minutes before testing with a skewer. If it comes out clean, the cake is cooked. Allow to cool in the tin, but turn out before completely cold. Enjoy with a good cup of your favourite tea.

Chocolate and nut brownies

For brownies, dry roast 50g crushed walnuts or hazelnuts, and add to the basic mixture. Cook in a greased rectangular tin. Cool in the tin before slicing.

Index

Thanks

Thank you to Alice Martineau, who taught me to always believe that anything is possible.

This book would not have been possible without the unending support of my two sous-chefs, Niki and Probyn Miers (otherwise known as my parents). They possess masochistic quantities of patience and kindness, and I could not have tested, cooked and produced all these recipes without them. They really ought to feature as co-authors. To my siblings for being great guinea pigs, albeit biased ones. To Sally Francis for being part of the cooking frenzy and joining in with gusto.

To my *Cook* photography team: Noel Murphy, Simon Gow, Sarah Tildesley, Claire Ptak and Hattie Eastwood. Noel, for his brilliant way of letting me just relax and get cooking. Simon, for his crackling wit and incredible ironing skills. Sarah, for the endless tips, tricks and ability to make my food look so beautiful. Claire, for those melting cakes and tarts, and for the fun. Hattie, for pulling in at the last. My kitchen became a hub of energy, work and filthy jokes during the photography - it never knew work could be such fun.

To Patricia at La Fromagerie, for letting us take so many great food shots in her shop and for always encouraging me. To Sarah Bilney for the same encouragement. To Trevor Smith in Winchcombe for supplying me with such delicious meat to cook with and to Hailes Farm Shop for such inspirational produce. To Tash Cubitt and her great recipe testing and to Chloe for being a Butt. To Fred, Ellie, Laetitia (the babe) and George for the Vacherin lunch. To Emily and Conor for game inspiration. To Laulie and Ted for letting me take over the kitchen at Doggetts; to Tiff and Charlie for eating the results. To Alex Garcia, for being there, even if there is Mexico City. To all my amazing friends for believing in me and being enthusiastic. To Genevieve for her injection of glamour into everything. To Lucy Cleland, the most loyal and supportive friend.

To Denise at HarperCollins for being an endlessly receptive and patient editor; Siobhán for her tireless copy-editing; Mark for his artistic super work; Nicky for the design. To Lisa Dwan, who masterminded the six months to launch with utter brilliance, and to Thomas Bunn, for all his amazing support. To Annabel Buckingham, from whom I've learnt so much. And to Antony Topping at Greene & Heaton, for being a constant teddy bear and agent extraordinaire. To Hugh, for being endlessly encouraging. To Richard and George, for being my first book team. To everyone I've forgotten; there will be lots.

Most of all to Mark, for never telling me to stop banging on about food and for being my rock.

Thank you everyone.

Bibliography

Ballymaloe Cookery Course, Darina Allen (Gill & Macmillan, 2001); *Casa Moro*, Sam & Sam Clark (Ebury, 2004); *Catalan Cuisine*, Colman Andrews (Grub Street, 1997); *The Cheese Room*, Patricia Michelson (Michael Joseph, 2001); *Chez Panisse Café Cookbook*, Alice Waters (HarperCollins, 2000); *Chez Panisse Vegetables*, Alice Waters (HarperCollins, 1996); *The Cookery Year* (Reader's Digest, 2004); *The Cook's Companion*, Stephanie Alexander (Viking, 2004); *English Food*, Jane Grigson (Penguin, 1998); *Fish*, Sophie Grigson, William Black (Headline, 2000); *Fish Book*, Jane Grigson (Penguin, 1998); *The Food I Love*, Neil Perry (Murdoch Books, 2005); *Fruit Book*, Jane Grigson (Penguin, 2000); *Good Things*, Jane Grigson (Michael Joseph, 1971); *The Kitchen Diaries*, Nigel Slater (Fourth Estate, 2005); *Le Gavroche Cookbook*, Michel Roux Jnr (Weidenfeld Nicolson, 2003); *Madhur Jaffrey's World Vegetarian* (Ebury, 1998); *Maggie's Table*, Maggie Beer (Lantern, 2006); *Mexico One Plate at a Time*, Rick Bayless (Simon & Schuster Inc, 2000); *Moro The Cookbook*, Sam & Sam Clark, (Ebury, 2003); *The Naked Chef*, Jamie Oliver (Penguin, 2001); *No place like home*, Rowley Leigh (Fourth Estate, 2000); *Relax, it's only food*, John Torode (Quadrille, 1999); *River Cafe Green*, Ruth Rogers, Rose Gray (Ebury, 2001); *The River Cottage Meat Book*, Hugh Fearnley-Whittingstall (Hodder Headline, 2004); *Seasonal Food*, Paul Waddington (Eden Books Transworld, 2004); *Soup Kitchen*, Thomasina Miers, Annabel Buckingham (Collins, 2005); *Tamarind & Saffron*, Claudia Roden (Penguin, 2000); *Vegetable Book*, Jane Grigson (Penguin, 1998); *Verdura*, Viana La Place, Grub Street, 2006); *The Zuni Café Cookbook*, Judy Rogers (W W Norton & Co, 2002)